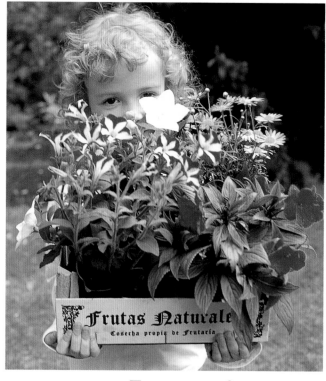

gardening
with kids

Catherine Woram & Martyn Cox

gardening
with kids

photography by
Polly Wreford

RYLAND
PETERS
& SMALL

LONDON NEW YORK

Designer Iona Hoyle

Commissioning editor Annabel Morgan

Location researcher Emily Westlake

Production Paul Harding

Art director Leslie Harrington

Publishing director Alison Starling

First published in the UK in 2008
by Ryland Peters & Small
20–21 Jockey's Fields
London WC1R 2BW
www.rylandpeters.com

10 9 8 7 6 5 4 3 2

ISBN 978-1-84597-589-0

A CIP record for this book is available from the
British Library.

Printed in China.

contents

introduction

I've got my family to blame for my obsession with plants and gardens. As a toddler, I'd play with worms, make mud pies or pluck rose petals from my mother's plants, mixing them with water to make my own perfume in old jam jars. Later, I would learn about fruit and vegetables from my granddad, a fabulous gardener who would unearth potatoes before my eyes – as a child it was like seeing gold nuggets appearing from the earth! He gave me plump gooseberries and blackcurrants to eat, which made my eyes water, and let me pick peas straight from the plant. Even now, I can clearly remember the overpowering smell of the tomatoes that grew rampantly in his little greenhouse.

Enjoying being in the garden as a child, whether I was playing, picking vegetables or growing plants in my own little patch of soil has stayed with me for life, and is a reason why I wanted to take up gardening for a living. Although few other kids will go on to become a professional, early exposure to gardening will sow the seed for a fascinating and rewarding hobby, and time spent outside is a far healthier alternative to sitting in front of the TV or computer screen.

Kids will love the many different projects in this book, which will expose them to lots of fabulous plants, from pretty flowers to curious insect eaters, and provide them with a gentle introduction to the technical skills needed to garden. The fun, colourful garden-related craft projects, meanwhile, will allow them to channel their creativity and keep them entertained on rainy afternoons, when gardening is out of the question!

Both the growing and crafting projects are quick and easy, and fun to put together. Although some growing projects require a little patience (for plants or seeds to grow), most of the craft ones will yield instant results that kids will find encouraging. Here's to the next generation of green-fingered gardeners!

Martyn Cox

gardening with kids

gardening with kids

Before children arrive on the scene, we treat our gardens as adult-only spaces for outdoor entertaining and relaxing after a hard day at work. The minimalism of these gardens is unlikely to excite kids, but every garden, no matter how small, has the potential to be a fantastic playground.

Safety first

Although you may be lucky enough to have a garden that is already child-friendly, many gardens need a bit of a tweak, both in terms of safety and to make them more stimulating. If you have very young children, then the most important thing is to make the garden a safe place. If you have ponds, fill them in until your kids are older. Alternatively, you could fence them off, or fix a decorative grille over the top.

Elsewhere, keep sheds or garages locked to prevent kids gaining access to machinery, tools or pest and disease controls. For complete peace of mind, always be in the garden with them and keep a close eye on what they are doing.

Add some excitement

If you are planning a child-friendly garden or adapting your existing space, then include plants that kids will find exhilarating. Large-leaved exotics, such as banana plants, make brilliant places to hide, while grasses and other tactile plants will become child magnets that just have to be touched and stroked whenever they head outdoors. Next on your list should be play equipment. A simple swing, sandpit, slide or activity centre will provide years of fun.

Give them their own patch

Find them a patch where they can grow their own vegetables, fruit or flowers. Children like their independence, and will get a thrill out of seeing their very own plants grow. To really give them ownership, help them to make a sign and paint their name on it, and allow them to manage the plot without your help or interference.

this page and opposite: getting green fingers
If kids are exposed to the joys of gardening from a young age, they will soon become hooked. There are many elements of gardening that will appeal to kids – some will like watching seeds develop into a plant, while others will enjoy studying insects, and some children will just like getting their hands dirty!

Top tips on gardening with kids

- Give them a decent patch of soil where they can grow vegetables or flowers – not just the damp shady spot at the back of the garden!
- Learn to relax, and let kids get mucky. It's fun!
- Teach them not to eat anything growing in the garden, unless you are with them.
- For peace of mind with very young children, make sure there is no in-built danger, such as uncovered ponds or dangerous machinery left lying around. To prevent them wandering off, make sure your gate is firmly shut and that there are no large gaps in the fence.
- Find space for play equipment and buy some garden games – these will provide hours of energetic fun.
- Turn your garden into an exciting jungle by adding some big, leafy exotics to your borders, such as banana plants or tall bamboo.
- Kids will want to spend all summer out of doors, so make sure they wear sun hats and use a high-factor sunscreen, which is reapplied regularly. Provide them with some shade or bring them indoors when the sun is at its strongest – usually between 11am and 3pm.
- Kids love mini-beasts, so make wildlife habitats and encourage birds by putting out food.
- Try to keep an area of lawn. It's great for playing games, rolling around or having picnics.
- Children are territorial, so give them their own set of garden tools to inspire them and get them started.

**this page and opposite above:
all kitted out**

Kids love being kitted out with pint-sized versions of the tools used by adults to maintain a garden. Look for scaled-down replicas that will fit snugly into a child's hand. Choose tools to suit the age of your children – plastic tools are perfect for toddlers, but older kids will prefer metal-bladed tools. When buying, check the quality to ensure they will last.

getting started

Being given their first set of gardening equipment is a memorable experience for kids, and is the perfect way to encourage their interest in the garden. It can be great fun to go shopping together so they can help choose their own set of garden tools. The result will be tools they won't want to put down!

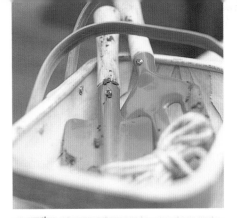

The starting point with any gardener, whatever their age, is to get equipped – you simply can't garden without the right tools. Fortunately, there are lots designed especially for kids and made from a variety of materials. Tough, round-edged miniature plastic tools are ideal for the very young, while longer-handled versions with stronger metal heads are perfect for older children. Most garden centres or DIY stores stock a good range, so it's not difficult to put together a first garden tool kit. Remember to keep it simple, as most gardening tasks can be carried out with a few tools (see box), and any special equipment can be bought as their interest develops.

Essential tool kit

Need to put a kids' gardening kit together? The important thing is to keep it simple, as most gardening can be carried out with a few key tools. Here are the essentials:

- hand trowel
- hand fork
- spade
- fork
- rake
- mini-wheelbarrow
- Dutch or draw hoe
- garden scissors
- watering can
- broom

What to wear

Although kids can garden in old clothes, so it won't matter if they get dirty or damaged, it is still a good idea to provide them with some protective clothing. A pretty floral fabric or PVC gardening apron is perfect for girls, while boys (and some girls) may prefer an apron with a fun bug motif. A pair of brightly coloured Wellington boots will keep their feet snug and dry, and kids should always wear a pair of gardening gloves whenever they handle soil or material like well-rotted farmyard compost. This will prevent them picking up harmful bacteria, or diseases such toxoplasmosis, which is caused by decaying pet faeces.

Storing equipment

As kids are quite territorial, give them somewhere they can store their tools. A brightly painted box in your shed or garage

this picture: give it some welly
A pair of Wellington boots is essential when kids are digging or splashing around in water. Children are attracted to boots in striking, primary colours or those with bold patterns printed on them – perfect for brightening up even the muddiest day.

would be ideal, especially if you (or they) paint their name onto it. Better still, give them complete ownership by finding space for a mini-shed or wooden play house in the garden, and allowing them to stash their garden equipment inside. You could even add plastic-coated hooks to the walls, so the tools can be neatly hung up after a session in the garden!

Preparing the soil

There is nothing more likely to put off a budding gardener than their plants failing to grow. To ensure kids remain enthusiastic it is important to teach them how to prepare the soil properly, so seeds germinate and plants thrive.

Being given your own patch of soil is a rite of passage, and many adult gardeners started off with their own little patch, where they grew flowers or vegetables. Creating their own garden is tremendously empowering for kids and, if given ownership of the plot, they will enjoy visiting it daily to carry out maintenance, such as watering or weeding, or to check on their plants.

If possible, give them a good piece of soil in a sunny spot, not a weedy patch in the shade, where nothing will grow – the

idea is to encourage them, not put them off for life! Ideally, it should be within easy sight of the house, and not too large or they may struggle to care for it – a 90 by 90cm square would be the perfect size for beginners. Edge the plot with pebbles, shells, bricks or lengths of log, and mark their territory with a fun sign painted with their name.

Unless you've given them recently cultivated soil, it will need some work before planting in spring. Start by removing any weeds, then dig it over with a spade. Next, rake the soil to leave a fine finish and walk up and down on the soil with your heels to compact it. Then rake again, removing any large stones that have worked their way to the surface. Three weeks before planting or sowing seeds, improve the soil by spreading well-rotted farmyard manure

over the soil and work it into the surface with a fork (remember always to wear gloves when handling manure). The best time to prepare the soil is in the autumn, but don't worry if you never got round to it – soil can still be prepared in spring.

Even if you only have a tiny garden or just a balcony, there's no need for your kids to be left out – the good news is that many compact varieties of fruit, vegetable, flowers and herbs will thrive in containers filled with compost. See page 27 for a list of fun plants that can be grown in pots.

below and opposite: perfect preparations
If you are lucky enough to have a large garden, your children will take great pleasure in being given their own little patch. They will also enjoy the responsibility of thoroughly preparing the soil from scratch, which will enable them to successfully grow a selection of their favourite fruit, vegetables and flowering plants.

this page and opposite: taking care of your soil

Many adults don't bother looking after their garden soil, considering it to be a bit of a chore, but kids will benefit from the exercise and revel in nurturing their patch of ground. If they are taught that improving the soil means their plants will grow better, then they will happily spend time preparing the soil. Teach your kids to dig over the ground, to boost the soil by adding well-rotted manure, to weed and to water, or to make their own compost by collecting kitchen waste and prunings. All of this work will pay handsome dividends when it comes to harvesting or flowering time, and they will want to do it all over again the following year.

Maintaining the garden

With a little bit of tender loving care, a garden will flourish, providing positive results that will fill kids with enthusiasm. From learning how to water properly to making a compost heap, kids will enjoy picking up the simple techniques needed to maintain their space.

Watering

Every plant needs water to keep it in good shape, but there is no simple 'one size fits all' rule as every plant and garden situation is different. Generally, ensure that plants do not dry out, especially seedlings or plants in pot, which will soon wilt when their roots have drawn every last drop from the compost. While plants are actively growing or bearing flowers or fruit, you may need to water daily, or even twice a day for some thirsty pots, such as hanging baskets. Let kids water their plants with a watering can fitted with a fine rose attachment – this gives a soft trickle, rather than an earth-boring torrent of water.

Feeding

Garden centres are full of dozens of different fertilisers, but the best thing to do in a kid's garden is keep the feeding regime very simple and easy to follow. All they really need is a liquid feed that's high in potassium, such as tomato fertiliser. This can then be added to water and poured onto plants to boost flower, fruit or vegetable production.

Mulching

A great trick to reduce the need for watering on permanent plantings of shrubs, perennials and trees (but not around seedlings or vegetables) is to spread a thick carpet of bark chippings or other organic material across the surface of the soil. Called a mulch, this thick layer prevents moisture from escaping from the soil, as well as looking good and preventing weeds from growing. You can use a similar technique with pots, covering the surface of the soil with shells, pine cones, pebbles or smooth tumbled pieces of coloured glass.

Composting

You end up with a lot of waste in the garden, so show your kids how lawn clippings, prunings and dead flower heads can be turned into compost. Add organic material in layers to the bin of your choice, and within months the spent material will have magically turned into compost. In a small garden, try a worm bin – these can be bought as kits and are ideal for most garden waste and vegetable peelings from the kitchen.

Pest control

To us they are annoying pests, but many very young kids think of slugs, snails and other leaf-munching beasties as cute garden pets – some even give them names and keep them in small boxes. Obviously you do not want all of their hard work to go to waste, so a degree of control (ideally when they are not looking!) is necessary. In the long run, it's probably best to take a tip from organic gardeners and learn to live with a few pests.

growing and planting

Many adults have started a lifelong fascination with gardening when young, raising cress on blotting paper or by sowing the pips from an apple core in the soil. Growing from seed is a magical experience for children, especially if you use fast-growing seeds that pop up in just a few days.

Sprouting seeds

Cast your mind back to your school days, and you may recall a basic lesson in botany when a teacher showed the class how seeds germinate. He or she would moisten a broad bean seed and drop it into a glass jar, while you would check it daily to see whether it had produced any roots or shoots.

Watching seeds germinate fascinates children, largely because it demystifies a process that usually takes place underground, letting them see how plants grow. It is incredibly easy to try this at home. Simply curl up a piece of kitchen roll into a cylinder and put inside an old jam jar. Moisten a bean seed (perfect, because they are fast-growing) and place halfway down the side of the jar, sandwiched between the paper and the glass. Pour some water into the jar and the kitchen roll will soak it up to hold the bean in place. Within a few days, you will notice the beans swell. This will lead to the seed coat cracking and the root appearing, later followed by the slowly unfurling shoot that carries the leaves.

Even more fun are edible sprouting seeds, which can be grown in a jar or a special sprouting device. Alfalfa, beet, chickpeas, lentils, mung beans and fenugreek are ideal, will appear in a day or so, and are perfect for adding a crunch to salads or sandwiches.

Planting from seed

Seeds are simple to grow, whether you decide to buy seed packets from a garden centre or collect your own from seed heads in the garden (check the plants aren't poisonous before allowing children to gather them). All you need to do is fill a pot with compost, firm it down gently to leave a level surface, and then scatter the seeds on top. Cover with compost (how much depends on the size of the seeds, so check the back of the seed packet for information), water and put them in a light place to germinate. Many seeds will

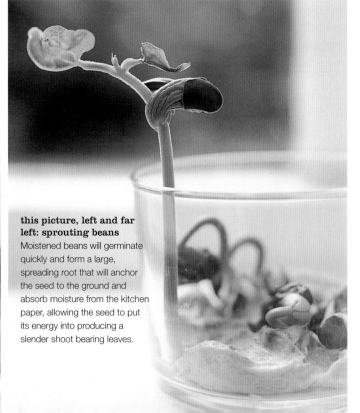

this picture, left and far left: sprouting beans
Moistened beans will germinate quickly and form a large, spreading root that will anchor the seed to the ground and absorb moisture from the kitchen paper, allowing the seed to put its energy into producing a slender shoot bearing leaves.

above and right: sowing seeds
Children love to choose seeds from the massive range sold in garden centres. It's also fun to save your own seeds. Show kids how to collect them from drying flower heads and store them in envelopes for sowing next year.

above and opposite: simple cuttings
Propagating succulent plants is fun and foolproof. Cut off a length of stem and put in a pot filled with gritty compost – it should root within weeks. Kids will enjoy making paper pots for cuttings with a pot-maker device.

left: repotting seedlings
It's easy to germinate seeds in the same pot, but as they grow into seedlings they will need a pot of their own, so they don't have to compete for nutrients and water. Remove the seedlings carefully, handling the roots gently, and replant them at the same depth as before.

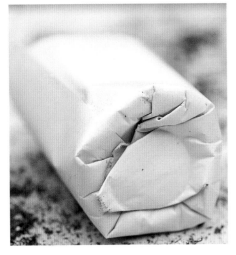

germinate more quickly if they are popped into a windowsill propagator, but don't worry if you haven't got one – a clear plastic freezer bag placed over the pot and secured with an elastic band will work just as well, and can be removed after the seeds have germinated. When the seedlings are large enough (several weeks later), they can be allowed to fully develop by giving them a pot of their own.

Buying plants

Raising plants from seed is great when you have fast-growing flowers or vegetables, or have patient kids who don't mind waiting several months for plodding plants to reach their peak. However, if you want to cheat or are itching to grow a plant that you can't raise from seed, then buy them from a nursery, garden centre or online specialist.

Go for plants that are vigorous, healthy and have no visible signs of pests and diseases. It also pays to be sneaky and lift the plant out of the pot to check its roots – if the rootball is a mass of congested roots that are spiralling round and round, put it back – pot-bound plants will have been in the container for a very long time, and the roots may fail to anchor the plant securely when planted. The perfect plant will fill the pot, but the roots won't be circling.

Planting

Although some plants are fussy, when it comes to planting you generally need to prepare a roundish hole that is slightly deeper and wider than the rootball. The surface of the rootball should sit at the same level as the surface of the soil. Remove the plant from its pot, put it in the hole and add or remove soil as necessary. Firm the soil and water well after planting.

Taking easy cuttings

An alternative to buying plants is to let kids grow plants themselves by making simple cuttings. Perhaps the most foolproof plants to try this out on are indoor succulents. All you need to do is snap a healthy leaf from a plant, and rest on the edge of a small pot filled with gritty compost. The cut end will soon form roots in the compost, followed by a new plant.

choosing plants

To nurture a child's interest in gardening, it's essential to let them get involved in picking plants for the garden. Growing varieties they have selected – with your help, to make sure they'll suit your garden – will help to give them a sense of ownership and they'll love caring for them.

Visiting the garden centre is a great adventure for kids, but for adults the endless benches crammed with so many plants can cause a serious amount of head-scratching. The tempting range on offer will often result in random impulse buys, and then it's only when we get home that we realise our garden can't provide the conditions the new plant requires.

Plants to suit your garden

There's nothing more disheartening than buying a new plant only for it to turn up its toes after being planted. To ensure plants thrive, choose ones that are suited to the conditions in your garden, whether it's in full sun or plunged in shade for much of the day. Equally important is to choose plants that will grow in your soil, whether it's clay or sandy, acidic or limey. Of course, there are ways of cheating – if you want to grow a plant that you know won't like your soil, you could always grow it in a container.

What to buy

There's little point filling the garden with delicate varieties that are easily damaged by inquisitive fingers or an errant football. Go for tough plants, so that children can touch, stroke or even scrunch up the leaves with their hands. Bananas, leathery elephant's-ears or soft, downy lamb's ears are all ideal and are able to cope with this kind of attention. Very young children will love to grow flowers in bright, primary colours, while slightly older kids will enjoy choosing and growing edible plants, which, apart from tasting great, will also help them understand about the origin of food.

What not to grow

There are loads of plants that kids can be encouraged to grow, but there are also several that are best avoided (see box opposite). Many well-known garden plants are poisonous, have vicious spikes or are covered in tiny hairs, which cause irritation to the skin when touched. Teach children what they can or can't touch and, as a general rule of thumb, don't let them eat anything without asking permission first.

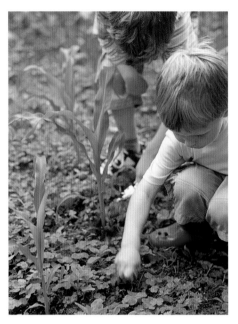

this page and opposite: decisions, decisions
Head to your nearest garden centre, nursery or DIY store and you will find shelves packed with fabulous plants. To nurture children's interest in gardening, it's essential to get them involved in choosing plants. Growing varieties they have helped select (with your help, to make sure they'll suit your garden) will give them a sense of ownership and they'll love to care for them.

What not to grow

These plants should be avoided when gardening with kids.

- *Aconitum* (monkshood)
- *Alstroemeria*
- *Brugmansia* (angel's trumpet)
- Castor-oil plant
- *Delphinium*
- *Echium* (viper's bugloss)
- *Euphorbia*
- Foxglove
- Giant hogweed
- *Laburnum*
- Lupin
- *Nerium oleander* (oleander)
- Rue
- *Solanum*
- *Zantedeschia* (calla lily)

above left and right, and left: beautiful but deadly

They are beautiful to look at, but lupin, foxglove, honesty and many other plants have poisonous seeds, berries, flowers or leaves, and are best not grown in a child-friendly garden.

plant lists

With thousands of different plants available to buy, it can be difficult to decide what to grow. To make life easier, here are themed lists of some fun and exciting plants that are child-friendly and will appeal to kids of all ages. Whether you've got a large garden or just a window box, there are some great plants to try.

Salad-bowl garden

- Lettuce 'Lollo Rosso'
- Spinach 'Bordeaux' (red stem, baby leaf)
- Lettuce 'Mizuna'
- Spring onion
- Cherry tomato 'Tumbler'
- Corn salad 'Pepite'
- Cucumber
- Lettuce 'Little Gem'
- Lamb's lettuce
- Edible carrot leaf (grown for leaves, not roots)
- Mustard
- Radish
- Beetroot 'Bulls Blood' (grown for its leaves)
- Tatsoi

left: funny face
Kids will love to make a funny face or pretty pattern out of the salad-bowl plants, fruit, berries and vegetables that they have grown in the garden. An old wooden seed tray, first lined with plastic and then filled with sand, will make a perfect frame for their home-grown edible designs.

Crazy fruit and vegetables

- Brussels sprouts 'Red Delicious' (purple sprouts)
- Chard 'Bright Lights' (mix of white, red, pink, gold and orange stems)
- Strawberry 'Maxim' (fruit as big as a small hand)
- Tomato 'Tigerella' (stripy fruit)
- Squash 'Turks Turban'
- Borlotti bean 'Lamon' (pink and white blotched pods and mottled beans)
- French bean 'Purple King' (dwarf purple beans)
- Cucumber 'Crystal Lemon' (round, yellow fruit)
- Aubergine 'Mohican' (white fruit)
- Carrot 'Purple Haze' (purple carrots)
- Sweetcorn 'Indian Summer' (white, red, purple and yellow kernels on the same cob)
- Sweetcorn 'Red Strawberry' (for popcorn)
- Raspberry 'Allgold' (golden raspberries)
- Beetroot 'Chioggia' (cut it open to reveal white and red concentric rings)
- Courgette 'One Ball' (round, orange fruit)

above: scaring the birds

After growing lots of delicious edible plants, the last thing you want is for greedy birds to take a share of your children's yummy crops! Try making a fun scarecrow, or suspend a string of CDs above the plants – you can use the free ones that are often given away with newspapers.

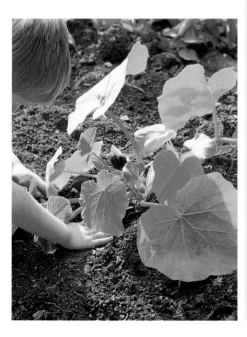

Fast-growing seeds

- Radish
- Carrot Parmex
- Rocket
- Cress
- Spinach
- Turnip Arcoat
- Beetroot Pronto
- *Nigella* 'Miss Jekyll' (love-in-a-mist)
- *Limnanthes* (fried egg plant)
- Nasturtium
- *Eschscholzia* (California poppy)
- *Cerinthe major* (honeywort)
- *Cosmidium*
- Sunflowers
- Annual poppies (not opium poppy)

Scratch and sniff

- *Stachys byzantina* (lamb's ears)
- *Salvia officinalis* 'Icterina' (variegated sage)
- *Salvia argentea* (woolly leaves)
- *Bergenia* (elephant's ears)
- *Stipa tenuissima* (feather grass)
- *Melianthus major* (blue leaves that smell of peanut butter)
- *Briza maxima* (quaking grass)
- Thyme
- Basil
- *Antennaria* (cat's-ear)
- *Helichrysum italicum* subsp. *serotinum* (curry plant)
- *Bellis perennis* cultivars (daisy)
- *Callistemon* (bottlebrush)
- *Convolvulus cneorum* (soft, silver leaves)
- *Coprosma* (shiny, glossy leaves)
- Bronze fennel (feathery foliage)

Giant's garden

- *Musa basjoo* (hardy banana)
- *Hosta* 'Big Daddy'
- Bamboo
- Tree fern
- *Fatsia japonica*
- Cardoon
- *Melianthus major* (honey bush)
- *Tetrapanax papyriferum* (rice paper plant)
- Runner beans (on wigwams)
- *Macleaya cordata* (plume poppy)
- *Verbena bonariensis*
- *Helianthus* 'Lemon Queen'
- *Dahlia imperialis* (tree dahlia)
- x *Fatshedera lizei*

above: water works
Children will be encouraged if the plants they grow thrive and flourish, rather than just limp along before turning brown and dying. Water is essential for a lush, verdant garden. To keep everything they grow in rude health, encourage your kids to water plants plentifully after planting, and let them check whether plants need watering on a daily basis.

Plants for pots

- Pansies and violets
- *Petunia*
- *Begonia*
- Nasturtium
- *Sempervivum* (houseleeks)
- Marigold
- *Pelargonium*
- *Cosmos atrosanguineus* (chocolate cosmos)
- *Fuchsia*
- *Brassica oleracea* (ornamental cabbage)
- *Lagurus ovatus* (hare's tail grass)
- *Solenostemon* (coleus)
- *Pennisetum* 'Purple Majesty'
- Heathers
- Box topiary shapes

Nature's garden

- *Buddleja* (butterfly bush)
- *Hebe*
- *Veronica*
- *Leucanthemum vulgare* (oxeye daisy)
- Runner beans
- *Dipsacus fullonum* (teasel)
- Forget-me-not
- *Stipa tenuissima* (feather grass)
- Sunflower
- Lavender
- Marigold
- *Nepeta* (catmint)
- Fennel
- *Sedum spectabile*
- Marjoram
- Rosemary
- Thyme
- Chives

this page: insect appeal
It's a great idea to turn your garden into a nature reserve by encouraging beneficial mini-beasts. Many plants (such as those listed on the 'Nature's garden' plant list above), garden features or feeding stations will act like magnets for ladybirds, butterflies, bees, birds and even small mammals, such as hedgehogs, and will allow your children to observe all these little creatures at close range.

growing

herb planter

Growing herbs is a great way to learn about edible plants, and they're a doddle to grow in a window box on a sunny window ledge or patio. For a never-ending supply of tasty leaves, all you need to do is keep on picking them.

1. Cover holes
Before filling your window box with compost, cover the drainage holes in the base. Use large stones or pieces of broken terracotta pot. This will allow water to drain away, but prevent the holes from getting clogged up with compost. It will also prevent compost spilling out through the holes and onto surfaces.

2. Add compost
Cover the base of your container with about 1cm of compost, breaking any large clods apart with your hands. Roughly level with your fingers to leave a smooth finish.

3. Arrange plants
Take your plants out of their containers and arrange them in the window box. Upright plants will look better in the centre of the container, while creeping plants are best tumbling over the ends. Once you are happy with your display, fill the gaps around the plants with compost, leaving a level surface about 2cm below the top of the trough. Firm around the plants with your fingertips and water them well.

HINTS AND TIPS
- Harvest your herbs regularly, to keep the plants productive.
- Always keep the container well watered – don't let it dry out.
- Chives, tarragon, parsley, rosemary, mint, sage and thyme are all perfect for growing in window boxes or troughs.

harvesting herbs

During late spring and summer, herbs make lots of fresh new growth, which is perfect for harvesting and drying. Store dried herbs in cellophane bags, and keep them handy in the kitchen. They also make great presents to give to friends.

1. Cut herbs
Select a handful of fresh, healthy new shoots and snip them off with a pair of scissors. To ensure the parent plant is left in good shape, cut just above a pair of leaves. Fill a bowl with cold water and quickly dip the shoots to remove any dirt, then gently dry them on paper towels.

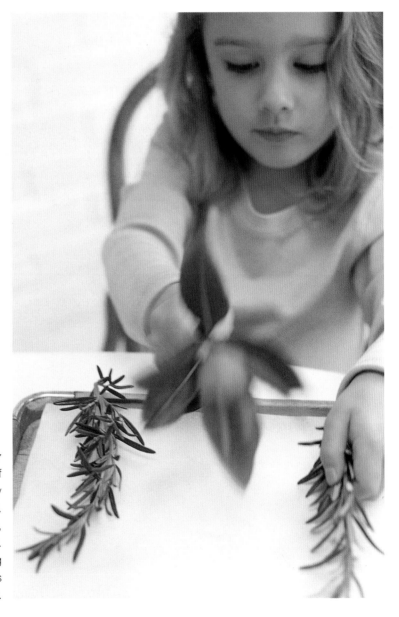

2. Prepare to dry
Cover a tray with a sheet of greaseproof paper and lay the shoots on top to dry. If you are drying different herbs, make sure they are not touching. Now put the tray in an airing cupboard until the herbs have dried completely.

3. Finish off

Carefully remove the individual leaves and put them into small cellophane bags. Fold over and secure the top of the bag to keep the contents fresh. Add a label, then store the herbs in a kitchen cupboard.

HINTS AND TIPS

• Herbs take several weeks to dry in an airing cupboard. They are ready when they snap easily, which means there is no moisture left in the leaves.

• Rosemary, bay, thyme, sage, marjoram, tarragon, basil and parsley are all ideal for drying.

• You can also finely chop herbs and freeze them in an ice-cube tray. Top them up with water and put the tray in the freezer.

cress eggheads

Creating these cute eggheads is really easy and fun. Fill them with fast-growing seed, then give the 'hair' a trim in a few days' time and add the yummy sprouts to sandwiches!

1. Prepare eggs

Remove the top from a hard-boiled egg by gently tapping around the outside of the shell with a knife (make a hole that is large enough for you to extract the egg). Scoop out the egg with a teaspoon.

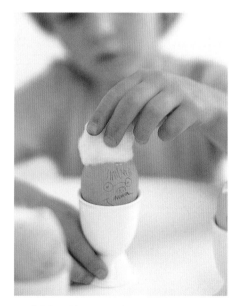

2. Draw on face

Hold the shell gently, and draw a face on the outside with a pencil. Don't press too hard, or you might break the shell.

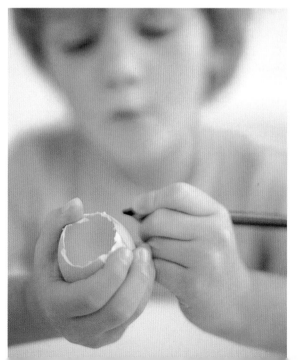

3. Add cotton wool

Gently push a handful of cotton wool into the eggshell. Pour in a little water and allow the cotton wool to soak it up.

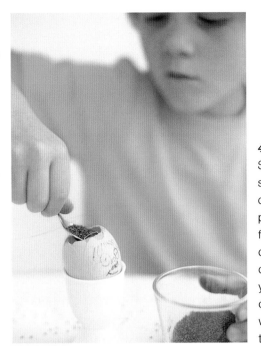

4. Sow seed

Sow a generous teaspoonful of seed over the surface of the damp cotton wool (we used cress and purple radish seeds). If you want, finish off the eggheads by using colourful paints to define the outline of the face you drew earlier. Now you can sit back and watch the crazy 'hair' grow, but remember to water the cress seeds every day so they do not dry out.

HINTS AND TIPS

• Make a body and feet for your egghead by cutting out a cup from a cardboard egg carton and using strong glue to attach short lengths of lollipop stick underneath. Paint them in jolly colours.

• Cut the 'hair' with scissors when it's about 5cm long.

• As well as cress, try growing super-fast red radish, mustard and garlic chives.

potato planter

Whether you like them mashed, roasted or baked, potatoes are an easy vegetable to grow in a large container. Plant seed potatoes in spring, and you'll soon be unearthing masses of tasty tubers.

★ **WHAT YOU WILL NEED**
• large planter, at least 30cm wide and deep (we used a metal dustbin)
• multi-purpose compost
• 3 x potato tubers per pot

1. Prepare pot
Most pots have holes in their base to allow excess water to drain away, preventing the growing potatoes from rotting. If yours doesn't, ask an adult to drill some in the base.

2. Sprout potatoes
When you buy your seed potatoes in late winter, you need to sprout them before planting. Place a single potato into the hollow of a cardboard egg carton, making sure that the end with the most eyes (little indents where buds will grow) faces upwards. Put in a light, cool place until the sprouts are about 3cm high. This stage may take up to six weeks.

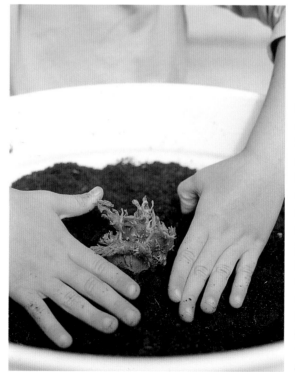

3. Plant sprouted potatoes
Add a 10cm layer of compost to your planter, stand a sprouted tuber on top with the sprouts pointing up, and cover with another 10cm layer of compost. Water well. When the shoots are about 15cm tall (which will take several weeks), cover the stems with compost, allowing the tips to just poke above the surface. As the stems grow, add more compost until you are left with a 10cm gap between the surface of the soil and top of the pot.

4. Harvest potatoes

Your potatoes will be ready for picking in midsummer, after the plants have flowered. Loosen the compost with your hands and pull the plants up. There should be plenty of potatoes attached to the roots and more hidden in the soil.

HINTS AND TIPS

• Potatoes will thrive in a warm and sunny spot.

• Keep plants well watered – never allow the soil to dry out.

• It's essential to keep on adding compost to cover the growing shoots, or your potatoes will be green and inedible.

• There are lots of potato varieties available, some of which produce larger tubers that need to stay in the soil until late summer.

butterfly basket

Bees and butterflies are good for the garden, and it's easy to attract them by planting a hanging basket full of their favourite flowers. Choose a sunny spot and hang from the branch of a tree or a bracket attached to the wall of your house.

1. Add compost
Ensure the basket liner has holes in the bottom for drainage – make some, if necessary. Put a thin layer of compost in the bottom of the basket, breaking up any clods with your hands.

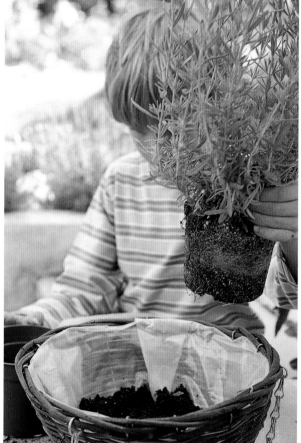

2. Start planting
Put the large lavender plant in the centre of the basket. Add or remove compost as needed, so there is a gap of about 2cm left between the surface of the rootball and the lip of the basket.

3. Pot-bound plants
Plants with a mass of congested roots will not be able to anchor themselves in the compost and will grow poorly. Tease the roots of pot-bound plants apart gently before planting them in the compost.

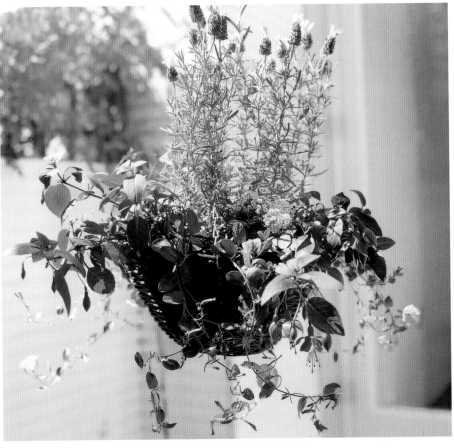

4. Finish planting

Plant your first fuchsia on the edge of the basket. Repeat with the two remaining fuchsias, spacing them evenly around the edge. Finish by planting one convolvulus, marigold and alyssum in each of the three remaining spaces. Firm the plants down well and plug any gaps with compost.

5. Water plants

To give your butterfly basket a flying start, water it well using a watering can fitted with a rose. This will ensure water is spread evenly across the container without eroding a hole in the compost.

HINTS AND TIPS

• Why not try some different plants in your basket? Bees and butterflies will also flock to veronica, hebe, bugle, cornflower, thrift, ageratum, heather and thyme.

• Water the basket regularly to prevent the compost from drying out – up to twice a day during hot weather.

• You can keep the display going for longer by pinching off any fading flowers with your fingers.

strawberry planter

Picking plump and juicy strawberries is a summer treat, and it's easy to grow your own in a special strawberry planter. For lots of berries, put the planter in a sunny spot and keep it well watered.

WHAT YOU WILL NEED
• large strawberry planter (with a drainage hole in the bottom)
• stones or pieces of broken terracotta pot
• multi-purpose compost
• strawberry plants (enough to fill all the pockets and one for the top)
• trowel
• watering can

HINTS AND TIPS
• Strawberries are thirsty plants and do need regular watering, especially during hot and dry weather.
• For even growth, it helps to turn the pot around occasionally, so each side gets some sunshine.
• You'll get better, bigger strawberries if you feed the plants once a week after they come into flower. Add a few drops of liquid tomato fertiliser to your watering can when you water the plants.

1. Add soil
Cover the drainage hole at the bottom of the pot with a stone to stop it clogging up. Add compost to just below the level of the first pocket and pat down with your fingers.

2. Plant strawberries
Remove a plant from its pot and put it into a pocket. Push compost around the roots, but don't cover the crown of the plant (where the shoots come from the soil).

3. Finish planting
Add more compost and plant up the other pockets. Finish off by putting a strawberry plant in the top and fill the gaps around it with compost. Leave a 2cm gap between the top of the compost and the lip of the pot.

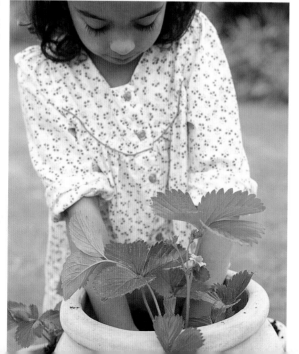

4. Water plants
Water well, so the roots are soaked. Water the top of the planter, not each pocket, as you could wash the compost out and expose the roots.

colourful annuals

Annuals will fill your garden with cheerful colour. Buy them as plants in early summer and they will flower non-stop until autumn. For a really fun, jazzy display, use your imagination and plant them in the most unusual containers you can find.

1. Add compost
Put a generous handful of compost in the bottom of a beaker. Don't worry about drainage holes, as annual plants only last for a short time.

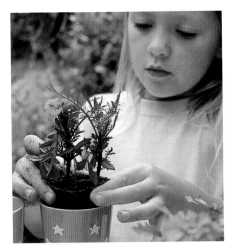

2. Plant up
Sit a plant on top of the compost. The surface of the rootball needs to be just beneath the lip of the pot, so add or remove compost as necessary.

3. Finish off
Use more compost to fill in any gaps around the edges of rootball and firm down with your fingertips. Water plants, but don't overdo it, as the beaker doesn't have drainage holes. Add some water, allow it to soak in, then test by pushing your finger into the compost. If it's thoroughly wet, you don't need to add any more.

1. Buy plants

You can find lots of jazzy annuals in the garden centre, including sunflowers, petunias, busy lizzies, pansies, violas, dahlias and marigolds. Buy a selection of the most striking flowers you can find to make a colourful splash in the garden.

2. Choose containers

Use your imagination and plant up lots of different types of container. Old teapots, jugs, saucepans and many other items found in the kitchen or around the house are ideal, and they can be arranged together to create an eye-catching display.

crystallised pansies

Real flowers make the prettiest of decorations for cupcakes, and they taste good too. Egg white and caster sugar is all that is needed to create these pretty crystallised flowers.

WHAT YOU WILL NEED
- fresh pansies
- plate
- paintbrush
- whites of two eggs
- caster sugar
- cupcakes
- cake plate or cakestand

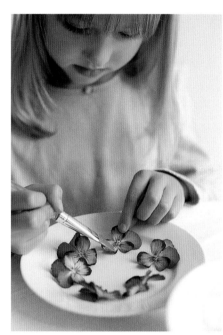

1. Paint on egg white
Using a fine paintbrush, carefully paint each flower with egg white. Paint no more than seven or eight flowers at a time, as the egg white dries quite quickly.

2. Sprinkle on sugar
Use a spoon to sprinkle caster sugar over the flowers, making sure not to add too much sugar. Leave to dry. The flowers will become hard and brittle.

3. Finish off
Use two or three of the flowers to decorate each cupcake. Serve on a pretty cake plate or glass cake stand.

HINTS AND TIPS
- There are many edible flowers, including roses and nasturtiums.
- Pick the flowers on a dry day – if they are damp, they will go mushy
- Pregnant women, elderly people and young children should avoid raw egg white.

cacti planter

Cacti are bizarre-looking plants that are covered in spines that help protect them from predators in their native environment. Many come from desert regions of the world, and it's great fun making your own miniature desert landscape by growing several plants together. Cacti are virtually indestructible, as long as they are given a light spot indoors and the occasional watering.

1. Apply undercoat

Apply a coat of white undercoat to the bowl, making sure that all the terracotta is evenly covered. It's easiest to paint the inside first. Then, when it's dry, turn the bowl over to paint the sides and base.

2. Paint overcoat

When the undercoat is completely dry, paint the bowl your chosen colour. Start with the inside, leave it to dry completely, then turn it over and paint the sides and base. For the best results, apply a second coat when the first is dry.

- large terracotta pot or bowl with a drainage hole in the base
- undercoat
- paint in your chosen colour
- three additional paint colours for decorative stripes
- paintbrushes
- stones or pieces of broken terracotta pot
- special cacti compost
- small trowel
- cacti (enough to fill your container)
- gloves
- strip of cardboard
- white gravel
- watering can

3. Add stripes

Jazz up your bowl by adding some stripes. We painted three concentric bands against the yellow background, using the ridges moulded into the bowl as a guide. Allow to dry completely.

4. Fill with compost

Cover the hole in the base of the bowl with a piece of broken pot or a stone to prevent the hole from becoming blocked. Start to fill with compost. Leave 2cm between the surface of the compost and the lip of the pot and firm with your fingertips.

5. Lifting cacti

Cacti are covered in tiny spines, so you need to pick up the plants carefully. When you are handling them, wear tough gloves and remove the plants from their pots by bending a strip of cardboard and clamping it around them. This way, you can pick up the cacti safely without getting spiked!

6. Plant cacti

Using a trowel, make planting holes in the compost. The plant's rootball needs to sit at the same level as the surface of the compost. Lower each cactus into its hole and fill any gaps with compost. Firm the compost with your fingertips.

7. Add gravel

Water the plants, then cover the entire surface with decorative gravel. We used white chippings, but you could use polished pebbles, sand or crushed shells. Spread a thick layer, which sits just beneath the edge of the pot.

HINTS AND TIPS

• From mid-autumn to the end of winter, water the cacti every three weeks, while from late spring to the end of summer, water when the compost starts to dry out.

• Many cacti enjoy bright sunshine, so put your cacti planter in the brightest spot possible, especially in winter time, when light levels dip.

alpine garden

Tiny alpine plants originate from mountainous parts of the world, where they thrive in well-drained soil among the rocks. It's easy to create your own miniature landscape by planting a selection of these mini-marvels in an old ceramic sink or a plastic trough.

WHAT YOU WILL NEED
- an old enamel sink
- gritty compost (a mix of 50 per cent John Innes 2 with 50 per cent horticultural grit is ideal)
- pieces of tufa rock (available from aquarium suppliers)
- horticultural grit
- watering can

alpine plants:
1 x thrift • 1 x houseleek • 1 x pratia
1 x bergeranthus • 3 x saxifrage
1 x stonecrop • 1 x rhodohypoxis
1 x sea campion

1. Choose plants
Garden centres stock a large range of diminutive alpine plants. Choose a selection of flowering and foliage plants and buy enough to spread across your sink. Don't buy too many, as you want to leave gaps between plants. We used ten plants, but you may need more or less depending on the size of your sink.

2. Add compost
Cover the plughole with a piece of broken terracotta pot or a stone, to allow drainage but prevent the hole from becoming blocked. Next, spread a layer of compost over the bottom of the sink.

3. Arrange plants
Arrange your plants, still in their pots, in the sink. If your container is to go against a wall, put big plants at the back and creeping varieties at the front to cascade down the sides. Small groups of plants often look best grouped together, such as the yellow saxifrages here.

4. Planting

Place your pieces of tufa in the sink. They look best when partially buried in the compost. Start planting in one corner, working your way across. Dig planting wholes, insert the plants, then fill the space around each plant with compost. Leave a 2cm gap between the surface of the compost and the top of the sink.

HINTS AND TIPS

• Old sinks are very heavy, so plant yours up in its final position – plants will do best in full sun or part shade.
• As flowers begin to fade, pinch them off between your fingers.
• Alpine gardens look great when the plants merge together, but you may need to thin out more vigorous plants to prevent them taking over.

5. Cover surface

After planting, add a blanket of horticultural grit to the surface. Not only does this look good, but it prevents weeds from growing and helps the soil retain moisture. If you spill grit onto the plants, you can remove it with a soft paintbrush. Now give each plant a good, long drink of water.

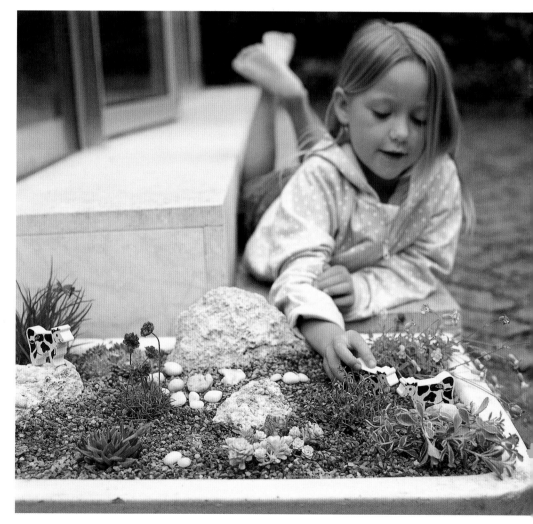

succulent tower

Houseleeks are the ultimate low-maintenance plant, as they don't need watering, pruning or any special care at all. They make a great feature for a patio when grown in a tower of different sized terracotta pots – try painting your pots first with exterior paint in your favourite colour.

1. Make base pot stable
Put a brick in the bottom of the largest pot to prevent the hole in the base of the pot from clogging up and to give the tower extra stability. Fill the gap around the brick with compost and firm down.

2. Stack second pot
Place the second pot on top of the first and put a stone or piece of broken pot over the drainage hole. About a quarter of the pot should sit below the lip of the first. Fill the top of the base pot with compost up to about 2cm below the lip of the pot.

3. Add top pot
Fit the last pot so that a quarter of it will be buried when compost is added. Cover the drainage hole with a piece of pot, then fill in the gap with compost and firm down. Now fill a third of the top pot with compost.

4. Add plants
Plant the first level with one type of houseleek. Make a hole with your finger and push the roots in. Plant the next layer and finish with the largest plant at the top.

5. Spread grit

Spread grit around each plant so the compost is covered. This prevents weeds from growing and keeps the bottom leaves of the plant dry so they don't rot.

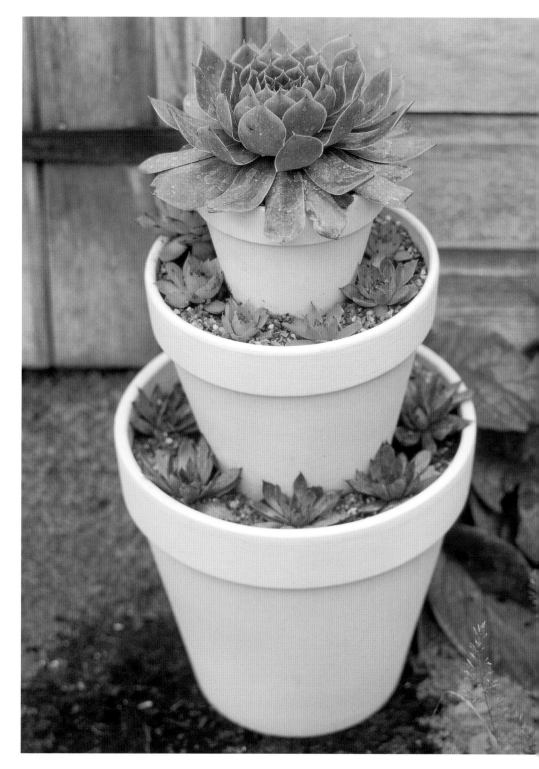

terrarium

You don't need a garden to grow lots of plants. Small houseplants can be planted together in large glass jars to make an eye-catching display that needs very little watering or care. These gardens in a bottle look great when placed on a windowsill or shelf.

WHAT YOU WILL NEED
- glass container (we used a Kilner jar)
- clay pellets
- horticultural charcoal
- multi-purpose compost
- long-handled spoon
- a selection of plants (enough for your container)
- watering can

1. Add clay pellets

Make sure the inside of the glass is clean (so you can see the plants!) and then slowly pour in your expanded clay pellets to make a 5cm drainage layer in the base of the jar.

2. Pour in charcoal

Permanently damp compost can become smelly, so add a thin layer of horticultural charcoal over the clay pellets, which will keep it fresh.

3. Fill with compost

Fill a quarter of the container with compost and firmly press it down with your fingers (if your wrist can't fit freely through the neck of the bottle, use the back of a long-handled spoon to press the compost down).

5. Water plants

Pour water gently into the jar until the compost is thoroughly wet. If you leave the jar open you will need to water the compost regularly, but if you close the lid the humidity inside the jar should provide enough moisture for the plants.

4. Plant up jar

Use the long-handled spoon to excavate small planting holes and lower plants into position. Firm the compost around the rootballs with the spoon. When you have finished planting, drop in some more clay pellets to fill any bare patches.

HINTS AND TIPS

• Lots of plants will thrive in a bottle garden. Choose tiny specimens of creeping fig, parlour palm, prayer plant, creeping Jenny, polka dot plant and mind-your-own-business. Avoid succulents, cacti, and plants grown for their flowers.

• If you are growing plants in a jar with the lid closed, the glass may occasionally become condensed and cloudy, so open the lid for a few minutes until it clears.

salad patch

A good way to start gardening is with your own patch of garden where you can create a bed of your favourite salad vegetables and flowers. Include a bamboo wigwam to provide support for climbing beans or peas. You don't need much space – a metre-square plot will do. It's a good idea to first create a planting pattern on paper before you plant in the soil.

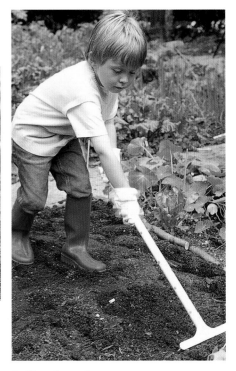

2. Tread down soil
Wearing a pair of wellies or stout shoes, walk up and down all over the entire bed, putting all your weight on your heels so you push down and compact the soil. This means there will be no uneven lumps or bumps in the bed.

3. Break up lumps
Rake the compacted soil backwards and forwards, so there are no big clods or lumps of soil and the surface is nice and smooth. Remove any big stones that have worked their way to the surface.

1. Spread manure
To give your plants a boost, spread manure all over the soil evenly and lightly dig it in with a spade or fork. It's important to remember to always wear gloves when you handle manure. Now roughly level the surface with a rake.

- well-rotted manure
- gloves
- spade/fork
- wellies
- rake
- 5 x garden canes
- garden twine
- hand trowel
- watering can

plants:
- 5 x runner beans
- 4 x tomato (tumbling variety)
- 4 x sweetcorn
- 1 x chard
- 1 x courgette
- 1 x nasturtium
- 1 x lettuce
- 16 x French marigolds

4. Push in canes

Make a bamboo wigwam at the centre of the bed. Evenly space five canes in a circle and push them firmly into the soil, to a depth of about 10cm (unless the soil is very soft, a grown-up will need to help, as it can be hard to push in the canes).

5. Make wigwam

Gather the tops of the canes together in your hand, cut a long length of garden twine, and then bind the canes together to finish your wigwam. Unless you are very tall, you'll probably need to ask a grown-up to help with this bit, as well!

6. Plant beans

Dig a hole with a trowel and carefully plant one bean seedling at the base of each cane. Wind the long shoot all the way around the cane, to help it start to climb (if necessary, you can keep it in place with a loosely tied piece of twine).

7. Water seedlings

Newly planted seedlings can wilt very quickly, so remember to always water them straight after planting. Use a watering can with a narrow spout and water the plants directly above the root area, so they get a really good soaking.

8. Add tomatoes

Now you've planted the beans, plant your tomatoes, putting one in the middle of each side of the bed. Dig a hole a few centimetres from the edge of the bed and plant a tomato. Repeat for the three remaining sides.

10. Finish off

Use the chard, courgette, nasturtium and lettuce plants to fill the gaps left between the sweetcorn and the wigwam. Now plant the marigolds all around the edges of the bed. Finish off by giving everything a good watering.

9. Plant sweetcorn

Excavate a hole at each corner of the bed and plant sweetcorn, ensuring that the roots are well covered with soil. Water well and repeat for each corner.

HINTS AND TIPS

• Slugs and snails will greedily munch their way through salad crops. You can hunt them down by regularly checking the undersides of leaves and removing them.

• You don't have to follow our plan exactly. Colourful lettuces, rocket, aubergines, spring onions, carrots and radish are all easy to grow, while peas can be trained up shorter wigwams.

• Apart from adding lots of colour to a bed, many flowers, such as nasturtium, calendula (pot marigold) and viola, are edible and can be added to salads, while French marigolds are useful to attract pesky whiteflies away from more precious (and tasty!) plants.

carnivorous garden

Watching the jaws of a Venus flytrap snap shut is fascinating, and it's just one of many insect-eating plants you can grow. They come from tropical climates, but are happy outdoors during the summer.

WHAT YOU WILL NEED
- plant pot (with a drainage hole in the bottom)
- undercoat
- paintbrush
- exterior paint in your chosen colours
- small sponge roller
- carnivorous plant compost (a special mix from plant suppliers, which contains no nutrients)
- carnivorous plants (we used Venus flytrap, sundew and two different pitcher plants)
- trowel
- saucer for plant pot
- rainwater
- watering can

HINTS AND TIPS
- These plants prefer rainwater to tap water and like moist compost.
- Some carnivorous plants are very tender, which means they can only be grown indoors.

1. Paint pot
Undercoat the pot and allow it to dry, before adding a light green overcoat. Use a sponge roller to add patches to create a jungly camouflage effect. Leave to dry.

2. Fill with compost
Cover the drainage hole with a stone to stop it from clogging up. Fill the pot with compost, leaving 2cm between the surface of the compost and the lip of the pot.

3. Arrange plants
With your plants still in their pots, arrange them on the surface of the compost to create an attractive display.

4. Plant up
Use a trowel to dig holes. Each plant's rootball must sit at the same level as the compost. Firm gently with your fingertips.

5. Water plants
Place the planted-up pot on a large saucer. Now, fill a narrow-spout watering can with rainwater and carefully wet the compost, allowing it to be soaked up before adding more. Stop when the water trickles through the compost and appears in the saucer.

making

painted pots

These plain terracotta plant pots have been painted in fun bright colours and decorated with bold contrasting spots. Use them indoors or out, or give them as gifts to friends and relations.

WHAT YOU WILL NEED
- terracotta plant pots
- saucer for paint
- assorted paintbrushes
- undercoat
- coloured paint
- pencil
- water-based acrylic varnish

1. Choose materials
Apply undercoat to the pots and allow them to dry thoroughly. Paint the inside of the pot with the undercoat to about half way down, so that the terracotta does not show. Apply a further coat if required.

2. Paint base colour
Apply the base colour of the pot to the outside and inside in the same way as the undercoat, and allow it to dry completely. If required, apply a further coat of paint and allow to dry.

3. Finish off
Use a pencil to draw the spots on the outside of the pot. Apply the contrasting paint, using a fine brush to fill in the spots, and allow to dry. Finish the pot with a coat of water-based acrylic varnish.

HINTS AND TIPS
- Broad stripes in contrasting colours also look great painted around pots. Once you have applied the base colour, use a pencil and draw them on the pot.

Terracotta flowerpot saucers can be painted to match the pots.
- Use a fine brush to paint vegetable motifs on the pots – red tomatoes, chunky orange carrots or green beans.

wooden nesting box

Plain wooden nesting boxes can be decorated with lollipop sticks and painted in soft pastel colours to create these fun boxes that will make a pretty addition to any tree or wall in the garden. Hang it in a sheltered spot, at least two metres above the ground.

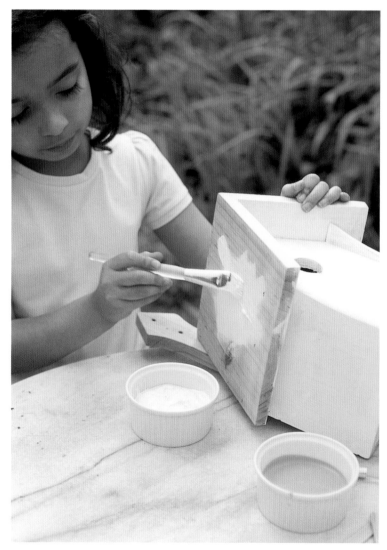

1. Apply undercoat
Use a large paintbrush to apply undercoat to the nesting box. Let it dry completely. Apply a second coat if necessary.

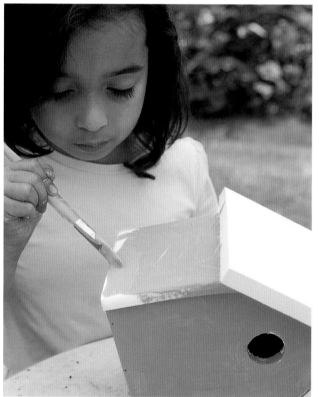

2. Paint base colour
Once the undercoat is dry, use a paintbrush to apply the first coat of green paint to the nesting box. Do not paint over the undercoat on the roof, however. Apply a further coat of green paint, if required, and allow to dry thoroughly.

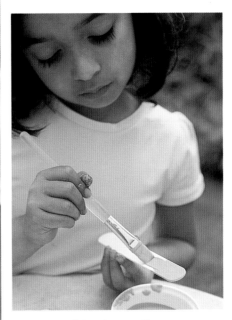

WHAT YOU WILL NEED
- plain wooden nesting box
- undercoat
- paint and paintbrush
- around 6 standard-size wooden lollipop/craft sticks for picket fence
- around 16 large wooden lollipop/craft sticks (depending on size of box) for roof
- strong glue and glue brush
- water-based acrylic varnish

4. Paint sticks for roof
Now take the larger craft sticks and divide them into two. Paint half of the larger craft sticks green and the other half cream. Allow to dry completely. Apply a further coat, if required.

3. Paint lollipop sticks
Apply undercoat to one side and the edges of the standard-sized lollipop sticks, then leave to dry. Paint the other side of the stick and leave to dry. Once completely dry, paint the sticks cream.

5. Glue on roof
Use strong glue to fix the large lollipop sticks to the roof. Glue them in alternate colours to create a striped effect, then leave the glue to dry.

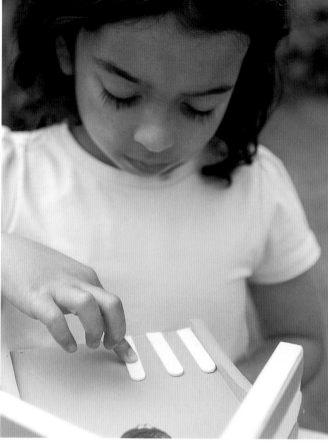

6. Attach picket fence
Ask an adult to cut four of the smaller lollipop sticks in half for the picket fence. Lie them along the base of the front of the nesting box and glue them in an even row along this edge.

HINTS AND TIPS
• Two coats of outdoor varnish will prolong the life of your nesting box. Varnish is available in both water-based and oil-based versions, but if you choose oil-based varnish it is recommended that an adult applies it, as it's more toxic.
• Try using shades of soft blue paint to create a seaside beach-hut nesting box for a very different, but equally cute, effect.

7. Finish off
Glue the remaining two smaller lollipop sticks on the top and bottom of the row of lollipop sticks horizontally. Finish the nesting box with one or two coats of varnish to make it suitable for outdoor use.

pine cone animals

These cute animals are made from pine cones and are decorated with felt ears, pompom eyes and pipe-cleaner tails. Different-sized pine cones will lend themselves to different creatures!

1. Draw ear shape
Draw an ear shape onto paper and cut out with scissors to make a template. Place the template on the felt and draw around it. Repeat for the second ear.

2. Cut and glue ears
Carefully cut out the ears. Pinch each one in half and put a dab of glue inside the fold to form a pleat. Allow to dry completely.

3. Make tail
Cut a length of pipe cleaner approximately 10cm long and loosely wind it around a finger to create a tail.

4. Glue on tail
Apply a dab of glue to the base of the pine cone and fix the tail to this. Press down gently to ensure that the tail is securely in position, and leave to dry completely.

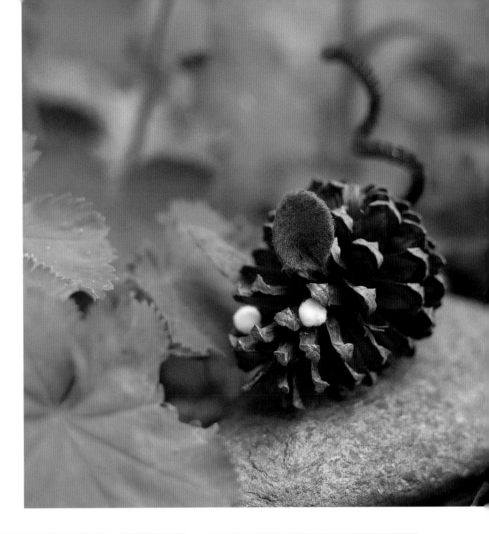

5. Attach ears

Put a small dab of glue on the base of the ears and push them in place between the layers of the pine cone. Use two miniature pompoms for the eyes and glue them just below the ears to finish.

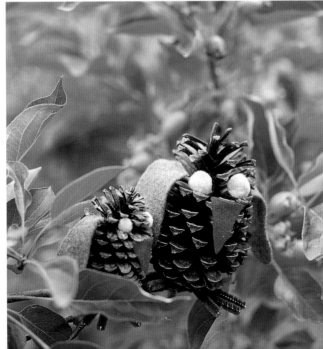

HINTS AND TIPS

• Use one large and one small pine cone to create this mother owl and her baby (left). Cut the wings from felt and use glue to attach them, and a triangle of red felt for the beak, to the sides of the cone. Use pipe cleaners to make the feet.

• Pine cones can also be used to make great Christmas decorations. Paint or spray them gold and silver, then attach loops or ribbon to hang them from.

pressing flowers

Delicate flowers such as pansies and daisies are perfect for pressing, and can be used to make pretty handmade tags or greetings cards to accompany gifts from the garden.

WHAT YOU WILL NEED
- flower press
- selection of flowers
- glue
- gift tags

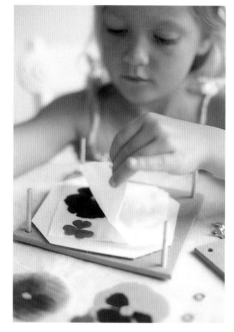

2. Remove flowers
After two or three weeks, carefully remove the flowers from the press. Pressed flowers are very delicate, so lay them on tissue paper to avoid damaging them.

1. Put flowers in press
Carefully position the flowers on the blotting paper provided with a flower press. Leave a gap between each flower or leaf. Screw the press together and leave for two to three weeks in a warm, dry place.

HINTS AND TIPS
- Pick your flowers on a warm, dry day, as wet flowers will go mushy when you press them.
- Dried flowers can be used to make many gifts, such as greetings cards and bookmarks. For a longer-lasting gift, apply a coat of water-based varnish to the item.

3. Apply glue
Carefully apply tiny dabs of glue to the back of the flower or, if preferred, use a very fine paintbrush to apply the glue.

4. Finish off
Turn the flower to the right side and fix to the gift tag in the required position. Using your fingertips, carefully press the flower flat and let the glue dry completely.

pebble birdbath

This fun birdbath is made using a broad, shallow terracotta plantpot saucer and a selection of natural polished pebbles. The birdbath is finished off by using grout to fill in the gaps. Place it on a low wall or garden table and watch the birds splashing around!

WHAT YOU WILL NEED
- paintbrush
- grey masonry paint for saucer
- terracotta plantpot saucer approx. 35cm in diameter
- selection of polished pebbles in assorted colours
- wooden craft stick to apply grout
- waterproof grout and adhesive

1. Paint saucer
Using a thick paintbrush, paint the whole outside and the inside rim of the saucer, and allow to dry thoroughly. Apply a further coat of paint if better coverage is required, and leave to dry.

2. Work out design
Arrange the pebbles on the base of the saucer in the required design. Take time to work out your pattern. We chose a flower shape for the centre of the plate and arranged the rest of the pebbles in the remaining space.

3. Apply glue
Using the end of a large wooden craft stick, apply a dab of waterproof adhesive and grout to the base of a pebble. Place the pebble on the saucer in your chosen position. Press the pebble gently in place, without using too much pressure.

5. Apply grout
Once the pebbles are fixed in place, use a craft stick to smooth the adhesive and grout over the pebbles and the entire base of the saucer. Now use a damp sponge to smooth the surface of the grout and wipe as much grout as possible from the tops of the pebbles. As the grout dries, remove excess grout with a damp sponge. When almost dry, use a damp sponge to wipe the surface, and when completely dry, use a cloth to polish the pebbles and remove any grout dust.

4. Glue on pebbles
Continue to fix the pebbles to the saucer using the waterproof adhesive and grout. When you have completed your pebble design, leave the birdbath to dry completely, preferably overnight.

HINTS AND TIPS
• For a more colourful version of this birdbath, try using the colourful glass nuggets that are sometimes used in flower arrangements. Find them at florists and in gift shops.
• Older children will have fun making crazy-paving-effect mosaic designs from pieces of broken china. Make sure that an adult breaks up any plates, as broken pottery has sharp edges that can cut little fingers.

fairy posies and daisy chains

This traditional garden activity will delight little girls of all ages. Miniature posies can be made for dolls or as gifts, while daisy chains make pretty necklaces and wreaths.

⭐ **WHAT YOU WILL NEED**
- tiny assorted flowers
- medium-sized leaf
- scissors
- raffia for ribbon bow

for the daisy chain and caterpillar:
- daisies
- scissors

1. Gather flowers
Pick an assortment of tiny flowers, such as daisies, from the garden and a medium-sized plain leaf in which to wrap the flowers.

2. Arrange posy
Arrange the flowers on the leaf, and fold the leaf around the stems of the flowers to hold them in place. Cut a length of raffia to secure the posy.

3. Finish off
Wrap the length of raffia around the base of the leaf and tie in a neat bow. Trim the ends of the raffia with scissors to finish off.

HINTS AND TIPS
- These miniature posies can also be dried to create longer-lasting arrangements. Hang the posy upside down in a warm, dry environment, such as an airing cupboard, for two to three weeks.
- When finishing off the pretty floral posies, you could use silk ribbon in toning shades for a more colourful alternative to the raffia. If you are having a tea party, put one tiny posy at each place!

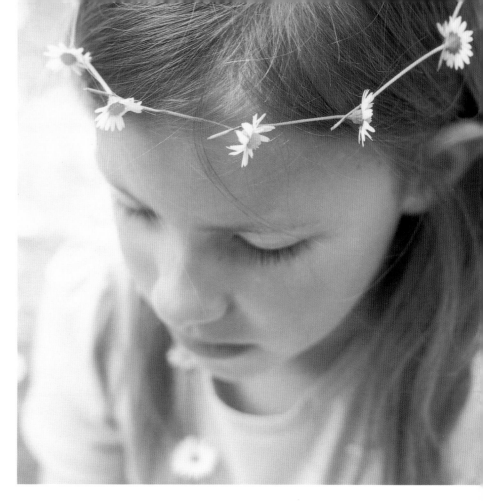

1. Collect daisies for chain

Pick a selection of fresh daisies. Break off the stems or snip them with scissors, so all the stems are of equal length.

2. Thread daisies

With a fingernail, make a small slit halfway down the stem of the daisy and push another daisy stem through. Repeat until you have the required length of daisy chain.

1. Prepare flower heads

Reserve one main daisy with a long, sturdy stem. Now take another daisy and pinch off the base to leave a hole in the centre. Thread this daisy over the main daisy's stem.

2. Finish off caterpillar

Continue to thread daisy heads onto the stem of the main daisy. You will need ten to twelve daisies to make a daisy caterpillar, as shown above.

elf house

This enchanting elf house will delight children of all ages. We used tiny twigs to make furniture and create a magical setting in the shelter of a garden tree and added tiny people made of felt.

WHAT YOU WILL NEED

- selection of twigs and bits of bark
- strong glue
- scissors
- felt
- 2 small pompoms
- pipe cleaner
- string for ladder

1. Make the chair

Cut ten 1.5cm twig lengths and two 3cm twig lengths for the chairback. Glue four shorter lengths together with one short length along the back for the seat. Glue two twigs to the front corners of the seat for legs. Glue the two longer twigs to a shorter length to form a chair back. Add a shorter twig to the centre as the support.

2. Glue together

Apply a dab of glue to the back corners of the base of the chair and stick to the back of the chair. Hold the chair together as the glue dries.

3. Make table

Take a small oval-shaped piece of bark and cut four 2.5cm twigs for the legs. Apply a dab of glue to the top of each twig and stick to the bottom of the bark approximately 2cm apart. Allow glue to dry thoroughly.

4. Cut out felt people

Cut a quarter-circle of felt measuring 4cm diameter. Wrap into a cone so the straight edges overlap by 2mm and glue along this line. Apply a dab of glue to the pompom and stick to the top of the cone.

5. Make arms

Cut one 6cm length of pipe cleaner and wrap it once around the top of the cone to form the arms.

7. Finish off ladder

Glue the next twig to the string approximately 2cm from the first and twist the string around the twig. Repeat to form the first side of the ladder. Using the same method, glue on the second length of the string on the other side of the ladder, making sure that the spaces between each twig are exactly the same. Trim the ends of the string to finish.

6. Cut twigs for ladder

To make the ladder, cut six 4cm twig lengths and two 20cm pieces of string. Apply a dab of glue to the end of the first twig and stick on the end of the string, wrapping the string around the twig as you do so. Hold the string and twig together as the glue dries.

HINTS AND TIPS

• Use longer lengths of twig to make a larger platform on which to sit the people and furniture.
• Tiny acorn cups make great bowls for the table!
• If you wish to leave the elf house outdoors permanently, apply a coat or two of exterior varnish to the platform and furniture to make it more durable.

hessian tote

Use natural hessian to make this practical yet pretty garden tote and use it to hold garden tools, seeds, plant labels and other gardening essentials. With its simple painted design of peas and carrots, it would make a great gift, too.

1. Cut out fabric

Cut a piece of hessian measuring 55cm by 18cm for the main bag, four 10cm by 10cm squares of hessian for the pockets, one oval of hessian (diameter 21cm by 14cm) plus two lengths of hessian measuring 24cm by 8cm for the handles. Use the selvedge of the fabric for the top of the pockets and for one of the longer sides of the handle sections to prevent fraying.

2. Decorate pockets

On the remaining three edges of each pocket, carefully pull away strands of hessian to fray the edges about 1cm from each side. Use a brush to paint a design on the pockets. Fix the paint according to the manufacturer's instructions.

3. Attach pockets

Take the length of the large hessian rectangle (allowing 1cm at each end for seam) and pin the pockets in place at evenly spaced intervals. Using green embroidery thread, make small running stitches to attach the pockets to the bag, leaving the selvedge edge open at the top.

4. Sew seam
Fold the piece of hessian with right sides facing, and stitch the sides of the bag together 1cm from the edge. Turn to right side and press both layers of the seam to one side. Using brown embroidery thread, stitch a row of running stitches along this seam to prevent it from fraying.

5. Stitch base to bag
Iron the Vilene fabric to one side of the hessian oval (it is advisable for an adult to do this). Now, with right sides facing, stitch the oval to the bag. Whipstitch around the raw edges to prevent fraying.

6. Stitch top hem
Turn the top of the bag 3cm to the inside and press flat with an iron, if necessary. Use lime green embroidery thread and running stitch to secure in place.

7. Make handles

Lay the two handle sections flat, turn the
top and bottom over by 1cm and press.
Fold the long edges 2cm to the inside,
making sure that the selvedge edge is on
top. Use running stitch to hold in place.

HINTS AND TIPS

• Try painting different garden motifs
on the pockets, or alternatively paint
on the child's initials or name.

• You could make a tote from
brightly coloured felt for a younger
child. Cut the felt with pinking
shears and the edges will not fray.
Jazz up the tote by appliqueing it
with leaf and flower motifs

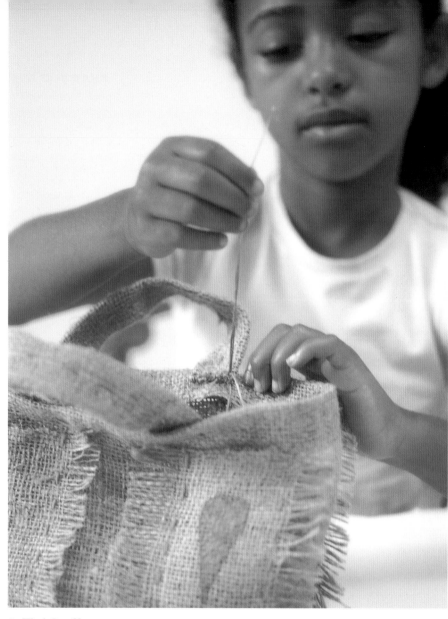

8. Finish off

Stitch the ends of the handles to the
inside of the bag approximately 12cm
apart. The handles are positioned along
the sides of the oval base shape, just
above the pockets. Use whipping stitch
to hold the handles in position.

lavender bags

These simple lavender bags are easy to sew and make lovely gifts for family and friends. Use a combination of pastel-coloured floral and spotty cotton fabrics for pretty vintage-style lavender bags.

WHAT YOU WILL NEED
• lavender
• floral fabric (each bag uses two rectangles fabric approx. 12cm by 20cm or a single rectangle 12cm by 40cm)
• pinking shears
• scissors
• cotton embroidery thread
• needle
• 25cm narrow white cotton ribbon per bag

1. Cut and dry lavender
Using scissors, carefully snip off long stems of lavender. Cover a tray with a sheet of greaseproof paper and place the lavender on top to dry. Put the tray in an airing cupboard until the herbs have dried completely. When dry, carefully pull off the lavender heads by hand and collect them in a bowl ready to fill your bags.

2. Cut out the bags
Using pinking shears to prevent the fabric edges from fraying, cut out a rectangle of fabric measuring 40cm by 12cm, or two rectangles measuring 20cm by 12cm.

3. Stitch bags
With wrong sides facing, stitch together the sides of the fabric and base of bag using running stitch and contrasting coloured cotton embroidery thread. The stitches should be no more than 1cm apart, so the lavender does not leak out.

5. Finish off

Lay the bag on one side and wrap the cotton ribbon around the bag just above the lavender. Tie a bow and trim the ends using scissors.

4. Fill with lavender

When the bag is complete, carefully fill it with loose lavender using a teaspoon. Fill the bag to approximately halfway up, but make sure it is quite plump and full.

HINTS AND TIPS

• Look out for pretty dresses or skirts in charity shops, which can be cut up to use for lavender bags.

• Felt hearts cut with pinking shears can also be filled with lavender. Stitch on fabric loops to make hanging lavender bags.

• Dried rose petals make an equally fragrant filler for these pretty bags. Dry them, then crush the petals gently and fill the bags, before tying with ribbon bows.

printed apron

This fun gardening apron is printed with a design of apples, created using the traditional potato-printing method. The familiar outline of the apple makes a simple, bold motif on the fabric when printed. You can use a ready-bought apron or, if you like sewing, you can make your own from cream calico and colourful bias binding.

WHAT YOU WILL NEED
- apple
- sharp knife for cutting apple
- kitchen paper
- fabric paint
- saucer for paint
- small sponge paint roller
- plain cotton apron

1. Apply paint to stamp
Ask a grown-up to cut the apple in half. Blot it with kitchen paper to remove excess moisture. Squirt some paint in a saucer, dip the paint roller in the paint and blot on side of plate to remove excess paint. Apply paint to the apple.

2. Stamp design on apron
Carefully place the apple cut-side down on the apron and press down firmly to make the imprint. Use a slight rocking motion to make sure that the paint has been applied to the whole area, but be careful not to smudge the print.

3. Finish off
Using the roller, apply more paint to the apple, then repeat the design all the way around the apron, as desired. Allow the paint to dry thoroughly, then iron the apron to seal the paint (following the manufacturer's instructions).

HINTS AND TIPS
• Try cutting different fruits and vegetables such as broccoli, carrots and cauliflower in half – they will all create interesting veggie motifs on fabric.

• This traditional printing method is fun and easy, and works just as well on cards and paper as on fabric – see the potato-print wrapping paper and cards project on pages 94–95, for example.

tin can windchime

Make a musical windchime using an old tin can and pretty glass beads to catch the light, then hang it from a tree in the garden. The tin is pierced with small holes for fixing the hanging decorations, so it's important to ask an adult to do this before starting the project.

1. Pierce holes

Ask an adult to pierce the holes in the tin before you start. You need two holes either side of the open end of the tin for the hanging wire. On the bottom of the tin, pierce one hole in the centre, four holes evenly spaced apart around the outside edge of the tin and four holes evenly spaced around the central hole. Now use a fine paintbrush to paint four narrow stripes around the outside of the tin, using the ridges of the tin as an outline.

2. Start threading

Cut a length of thread approximately 20cm long and attach one of the metal bells to the bottom, knotting it several times to secure. Begin threading four glass beads onto the string.

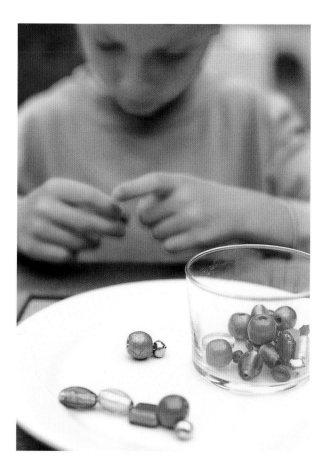

WHAT YOU WILL NEED
• Clean tin can with one end removed
• bradawl for punching holes
• Fine paintbrush
• Acrylic paint for stripes
• strong thread
• scissors
• 5 small jingle bells
• 20 large glass beads
• 9 small beads
• 1 metal clapper
• four tubular chimes
• 30cm fine wire for hanging

4. Thread on clapper

Take a length of thread approximately 20cm long and attach a bell to the end. Knot securely in place. Thread on the metal clapper, so that it hangs from the bottom of the cotton, just above the bell.

5. Thread on chimes

Cut a piece of thread approximately 30cm long. Double it, and knot the ends. Now thread it through the hole in the tubular chime and pull through so that it forms a loop.

3. Tie on bells

Repeat until you have made four bead lengths. We used pretty coloured glass beads, but you could use varnished wood beads for a more natural effect.

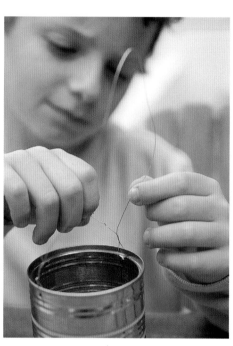

6. Tie on thread

The tubular chimes, clapper and beaded decorations are all attached to the inside of the tin by feeding the thread through the holes in the tin base and pulling through. The clapper must go through the central hole in the bottom of the tin and the tubular chimes around this. Finally, thread the beaded decorations through the outside holes.

HINTS AND TIPS

• Both wooden and metal windchime kits can be found in craft shops or on the internet, allowing you to add your own decorations to finish it off.

• Alternatively, you could take an old windchime to pieces and reuse the different parts, along with some pretty new beads and bells, to create our tin can windchime.

7. Fix wire handle

Thread a 30cm length of fine wire through the two holes punched in the sides of the top (open) end of the tin. Twist the wire around itself to secure in place. This is the loop from which to hang your windchime.

8. Finish off

Gather all the pieces of thread together, push the ends through a bead, and knot securely. The bead will prevent the pieces of thread slipping through the hole in the base.

pretty seed packets

It's fun and satisfying harvesting your own seeds and then packaging them for the following year in these pretty decorated envelopes. You could also give them to family and friends.

WHAT YOU WILL NEED

- small brown envelopes
- coloured pencils
- hole punch
- seeds
- raffia ribbon (approx. 25cm per packet)
- scissors

1. Decorate envelope
Decorate the edges of the front of the envelope with pretty designs such as wavy lines and and tiny polka dots.

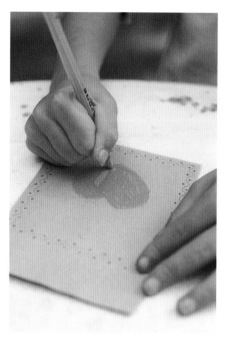

2. Draw on design
Now draw the shape of a flower or vegetable, depending on what seeds are in the envelope, and fill in the design using the colouring pencils. You may like to add the name of the seeds in your best handwriting.

3. Punch holes
Use a hole punch to make two holes at the top of the envelope, just where the flap is situated. Now carefully put the seeds in the envelope, and seal it closed.

4. Finish off
Thread the raffia through the two punched holes and tie in a decorative bow. Trim the ends of the raffia with scissors to finish.

HINTS AND TIPS
• Wrap tiny seeds in a piece of tissue paper and seal with tape before placing in the envelope.
• These envelopes would also look great decorated with potato-print designs – see pages 94–95.
• Look up on the internet the Latin names for the plants and write them on the front in your very best handwriting!

potato printing

Home-grown potatoes are not only delicious to eat, but can also be used for fun craft projects such as printing. You can even make your own wrapping paper and greeting cards by using a cut potato to stamp on a simple leaf-shaped design.

WHAT YOU WILL NEED
- medium-sized potato
- kitchen paper
- paint
- paintbrush
- brown wrapping paper
- card label for gift tag

1. Cut design

Ask an adult to cut the potato in half and carve out the leaf shape. Blot the potato with kitchen paper to remove excess moisture. Apply paint to the leaf motif using a paintbrush.

2. Print pattern

Carefully press the potato onto the paper to print the leaf design. Use a slight rocking motion to make sure that all the paint has been applied to the whole area.

3. Finish off

Repeat the design all over the paper at regular spacings, and allow the paper to dry thoroughly. Print a single leaf motif on greetings cards and gift tags to coordinate with your pretty wrapping paper.

HINTS AND TIPS

- Potato printing works equally well on fabric using fabric paints – see our printed apron on pages 86–87, which would look great in a potato print, too.

- Using a cookie cutter, make a star shape on the potato, then use this stamp to make your own fun Christmas wrapping paper and cards. Try using festive red paint on white paper.

birdseed feeder

Attract wild birds to your garden with this fun birdseed feeder. We made it from an onion squash, which was then decorated with cloves and filled with a generous heap of birdseed. Hang it from a tree in your garden and watch the birds tuck in!

WHAT YOU WILL NEED
- onion squash or small pumpkin
- bradawl (for piercing holes in squash)
- dried cloves
- scissors
- string
- small nail
- 1 packet suet
- saucepan
- birdseed mix
- spoon

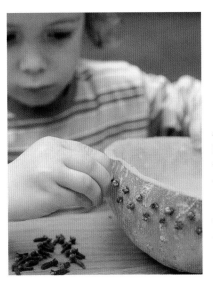

1. Cut squash in half
Ask an adult to cut the squash in half and scoop out the flesh from the inside (the seeds can be used to make the necklace on pages 100–101). The holes for the cloves are pierced using a bradawl, so it is advisable for an adult to do this. Insert the cloves around the edge of the squash in two parallel rows.

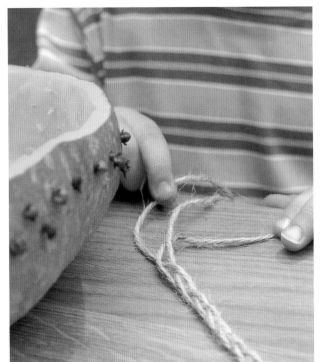

2. Plait string
Cut six 1m-long pieces of string. Take three strands and knot them together at one end. Start plaiting the string (it may be easier if someone helps you by holding the knotted end). When the first length is finished, plait the remaining three lengths to form the second hanging loop.

3. Fix hanging loops
Turn the squash upside down. Lay the plaited string in an 'X' across the base. Ask an adult to push in a nail to hold the string in place.

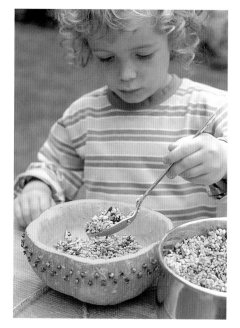

4. Finish off

Melt the packet of suet in a saucepan,
until it becomes liquid. Add the birdseed
and stir until the mix becomes firm.
Carefully spoon the mixture into the
squash bowl. Tie the ends of the string
around a branch of a tree, and trim the
ends using scissors.

HINTS AND TIPS

• For a more permanent bird
feeder, use a small wooden bowl
and ask an adult to drill four holes
just below the rim. Suspend from
plaited string hanging loops, and fill
with the seed and suet mix.
• Use the birdseed mix to fill nylon
net bags that peanuts or garlic are
sold in. Pour in the seed mix and
hang from a tree in the garden.

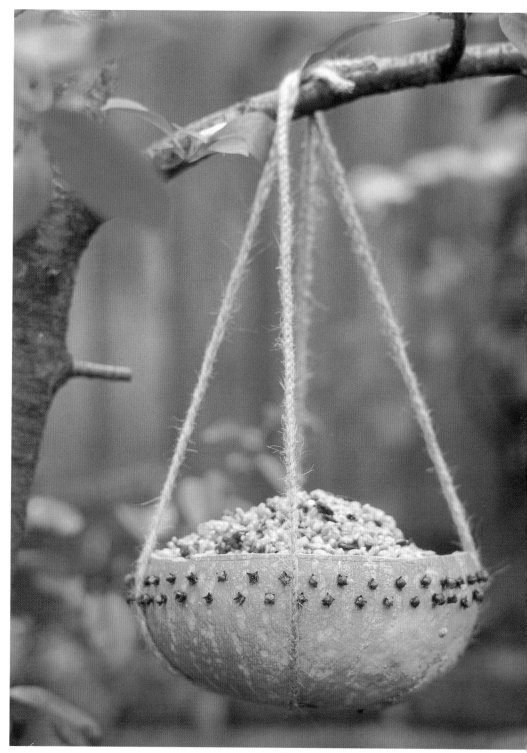

peanut heart

Peanuts can be easily pierced and threaded onto wire to create fun-shaped bird feeders that our feathered friends will appreciate in the winter months. We finished the feeder with a raffia bow to create a pretty and practical garden ornament.

WHAT YOU WILL NEED
• peanuts
• wooden skewer or bradawl for piercing holes
• strong wire
• raffia for bow
• twine for hanging loop (approx. 20cm)

1. Pierce holes in peanuts
Ask an adult to pierce the holes in the nuts using a wooden skewer or bradawl. You will need approximately 60 peanuts for one peanut heart.

HINTS AND TIPS
• It is recommended that an adult pierces the holes in the peanuts, as the pointed ends of the skewer or bradawl can be very sharp.
• For variety, try experimenting with different wire shapes, such as circles and ovals. Both would make ideal bird feeders.
• This peanut heart makes a great gift for any bird-loving relatives!

2. Thread peanuts
Fold the wire in half to create the 'V' shape of the base of the heart. Begin threading peanuts onto the wire. Each side needs around 30 peanuts.

3. Finish off
Ask an adult to bend each side of the heart into a curve to form a heart shape and twist the wire to fix the ends in place. Now tie a raffia bow at the top of the heart to cover the wire ends. Cut a 20cm length of twine to form the hanging loop, and suspend your bird feeder from a branch in the garden.

seed necklace

When it's too cold or wet to play outside, why not make your own jewellery from dried pumpkin seeds and sycamore wings threaded on cotton? It's a great way of using up the seeds from the carved Halloween pumpkin project on pages 102–103.

It's a great way of using up the seeds from the carved Halloween pumpkin project on pages 102–103.

WHAT YOU WILL NEED
- spoon
- pumpkin seeds
- bowl of warm water
- colander
- tray
- tea towel
- needle for making holes
- cotton thread
- sycamore wings

1. Remove seeds
Using a spoon, loosen the pumpkin flesh, then scoop out the flesh and seeds from the middle, using your hands.

2. Wash them
Put all the seeds in a bowl of warm water and leave to soak for a couple of hours so that the flesh comes away from the seeds. Carefully pick out the seeds and place in a colander.

3. Rinse seeds
When all the seeds are in the colander, run it under a tap to remove any remaining vestiges of pumpkin flesh.

4. Dry seeds
Lay out the seeds in rows on a tray covered with a clean tea towel. Leave in a warm dry place until the seeds have dried out. This can take up to a week.

4. Pierce holes

When the seeds are dry, use a needle to pierce holes through each seed ready for threading onto the necklace. It is advisable for an adult to carry out this task for younger children.

5. Thread on seeds

Thread the cotton thread on the needle and knot the ends. Begin threading the seeds and intersperse them with sycamore wings. When threading is complete, tie the ends of the thread in a knot to finish.

HINTS AND TIPS

To create matching bracelets, cut shorter lengths of fine elastic and thread on the pumpkin seeds then knot the ends. These make great presents!

• Paint the pumpkin seeds in a variety of pretty colours after they have been dried.
• Intersperse small wooden beads in coloured or natural finishes with the seeds for a more decorative necklace.

pumpkin lantern

This fun carved Halloween pumpkin looks more friendly than spooky! He's been given a pointy parsnip nose and a thick head of carrot-frond 'hair'. Fill him with tealights and leave him by the door to greet trick-or-treaters, or use him as a table centrepiece.

WHAT YOU WILL NEED
- large pumpkin
- sharp knife
- ice-cream scoop or spoon for scooping
- felt-tip pen
- parsnip for nose
- carrot fronds for hair

1. Scoop out seeds
Ask an adult to cut the top off the pumpkin using a sharp knife. Scoop out the flesh and seeds using an ice-cream scoop or a large spoon.

2. Draw on face
Draw eyes, nose and a mouth onto the pumpkin using a felt-tip pen. Ask an adult to cut out the shapes using a sharp knife.

3. Insert nose
Push the thick end of the parsnip into the nose hole to make a nose. Cut the fronds from the carrots to prepare the hair.

HINTS AND TIPS
- Set aside the pumpkin seeds to make pretty necklaces, as shown on pages 100–101. The seeds will need to be thoroughly washed and dried first.
- The pumpkin flesh can also be used to make delicious pumpkin soup and yummy pumpkin pie to serve to guests at Halloween!

4. Finish off
Lay the carrot fronds around the top of the pumpkin to make the hair. Insert tealights inside the pumpkin and ask an adult to light them. Now place the pumpkin on a pile of dried leaves by the front door or on the dining table.

scarecrow

Children will love making this friendly scarecrow and dressing it up in an assortment of their old clothes. When placed in the centre of the vegetable patch, it will hopefully deter rascally birds from eating their home-grown produce!

1. Make head
To make the scarecrow's head, cut a piece of hessian measuring 40cm by 55cm. With right sides facing, fold the fabric in half along the longest edge, then stitch along this edge 1.5cm from the raw edge.

2. Stuff head
Turn the hessian right side out. Tie a piece of string around the top of the hessian and knot tightly. Gently pull strands of the hessian to make a frayed edge. Now stuff the hessian head with straw until it is firm and full.

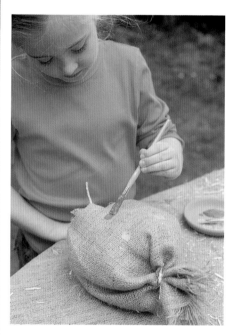

3. Paint on face
Use a paintbrush to paint the eyes and mouth on the front of the hessian to create the scarecrow's face. Allow the paint to dry thoroughly.

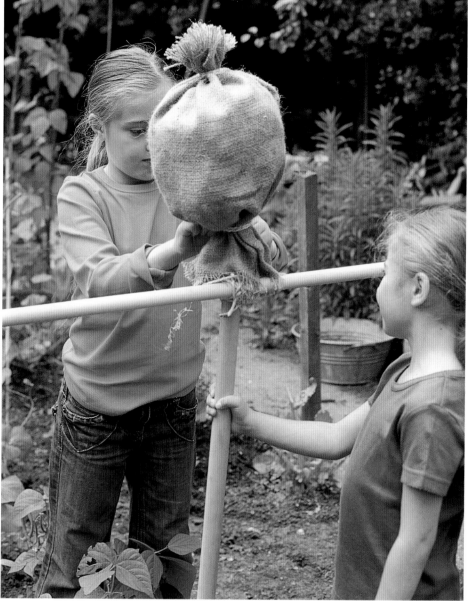

4. Make frame

Lay the longer wooden dowel on the ground and place the shorter one across it, approx. 40cm down from the top, to form a cross shape. Tie a length of string around the cross, wrapping it securely to hold the dowels in place.

5. Fix frame in ground

Push the dowel into the ground. You may have to dig a hole in the earth and then pat the earth firmly around the base of the dowel. Place the open end of the scarecrow's head over the dowel, and tie the base with string to secure it.

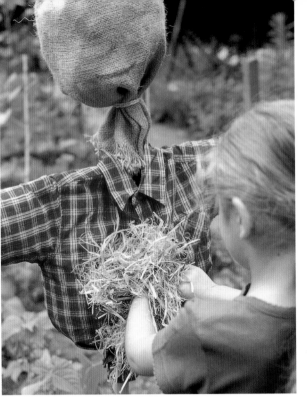

6. Dress scarecrow

Unbutton the shirt and put it on the scarecrow. Tightly tie a length of string around the bottom. This will prevent the straw stuffing from falling out of the shirt.

7. Stuff with straw

Stuff the shirt with straw in the arms and body to pad out the fabric and form the scarecrow shape. Continue to fill the shirt until the body is nice and plump.

HINTS AND TIPS

• An upturned terracotta flowerpot makes a fun head for a scarecrow and can easily be painted with a cheeky face. Make sure that the hole in the pot is big enough to allow the dowelling through.

• Use your own old clothes to dress up your scarecrow, or look out for clothes in charity shops.

• Deter particularly persistent birds by hanging shiny CDs from the end of the scarecrow's arms.

8. Finish off

Place the dungarees on the scarecrow (you may find it easier to cut a hole in the seat of the dungarees to thread the dowel through). Now stuff the legs of the dungarees with more straw. Place a jaunty straw hat on the scarecrow's head to finish.

harvest wreath

Decorate a ready-made wreath with your own dried leaves to create a decorative harvest wreath to hang on the wall or front door. Collect a variety of attractive, different-coloured leaves in autumn and use a flower press or large book to press them flat.

★ WHAT YOU WILL NEED
- dried leaves
- heart-shaped wreath
- glue
- dried seedheads and sycamore wings
- 25cm red gingham ribbon

1. Collect and dry leaves
Collect leaves for drying, making sure they are not damp. Place them between layers of paper in a thick book or flower press and leave for two or three weeks until dry. Put a dab of glue on the back of each leaf, and attach to the heart wreath.

2. Glue on leaves
Continue to glue leaves to the wreath and add sycamore wings and dried seedheads at regular intervals. Allow the glue to dry completely.

3. Finish off
Thread the gingham ribbon through the top of the heart wreath. Then tie in a knot so you have a hanging loop to suspend the wreath from.

HINTS AND TIPS
- For a more festive wreath, paint or spray the leaves using gold and silver paint as used for our Christmas wreath overleaf (pages 110–111).

- Pretty, brightly coloured berries can also be dried and used for added interest on the harvest wreath, but make absolutely sure they are not of a poisonous variety.

christmas wreath

Delicately shaped dried leaves, nuts and seedheads are painted silver and gold and used to adorn this stunning Christmas wreath, which will grace any front door during the festive season.

1. Dry and paint leaves
Gather leaves to dry from the garden or your local park. Lay them between layers of paper in a thick book or a flower press and leave for two to three weeks until dry. When dry, paint the leaves gold and silver and allow to dry. If necessary, apply a further coat of paint for even coverage.

2. Paint nuts and seedheads
Take the nuts and seedheads and paint them gold and silver using a fine paintbrush. Leave them to dry alongside the painted leaves.

3. Glue on leaf
Apply dabs of glue to the back of a leaf and place it in position on the wreath. Press down gently on the leaf to attach it to the wreath.

4. Attach rest of leaves

Take another leaf and apply glue to the back before sticking it to the wreath. Continue with this process until all the painted leaves are glued to the wreath.

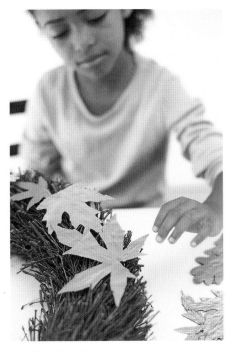

5. Finish off

Add the nuts and seedheads. Wrap the ribbon round the top of the wreath and tie in a bow. To finish, add a length of string to hang the wreath from.

HINTS AND TIPS

• It may be easier to use a hot glue gun to attach the seedheads and nuts. It is recommended that an adult uses the glue gun if younger children are working on this project.

• Miniature pine cones look great on Christmas wreaths too. Paint them silver and gold, just like the seedheads, and stick them on using a hot glue gun.

• For a rustic Scandinavian look, paint the leaves red and white.

twig decorations

These delicate-looking star decorations are made from thin twigs gathered from the garden or the park, painted silver and tied together with fine wire. The twig stars look pretty suspended from a mantelpiece or hung in groups on a Christmas tree.

WHAT YOU WILL NEED
- thin twigs
- silver paint
- fine paintbrush
- fine wire for tying
- scissors
- silver cotton or nylon thread for hanging loops

1. Apply paint
Choose three 10cm-long twigs and paint them silver. Allow to dry thoroughly. If required, apply a second coat of paint for even coverage and leave to dry.

2. Form star shape
Lay the three twigs one on top of each other to form a star shape. Cut a length of fine wire and bind it round the twigs to hold the star in place. Wrap the wire over the twigs several times, so that they are completely secure.

3. Attach hanging loop
Cut a length of thread for the hanging loop and fold in half. Wrap it round one 'arm' of the star, thread the ends back through the loop, and pull to attach the thread to the twig. Knot the two loose ends together to form a hanging loop.

HINTS AND TIPS
- Try painting the twig stars red and white and suspending the decorations from branches in a large jug for a pretty and festive table display.

- Once the twigs have been painted, apply a thin line of PVA glue along each twig, hold them over a plate or piece of newspaper and sprinkle with gold or silver glitter for more sparkly decorations.

outdoor fun

treasure hunts

A garden full of towering trees, shrubs or leafy exotics, with narrow paths cut through the display of plants, makes an exciting place for scavenger hunts or to follow clues that lead to a hidden treasure trove!

Scavenger hunts

Scavenger hunts are great fun and very easy to set up. All you need to do is spend a few minutes walking around the garden and putting together a list of objects that you can challenge the children to find. Although this is an ideal game to play at parties or to keep groups of kids entertained during the school holidays, it can also be played by a child on their own. Pine cones, fruit, feathers, shells, coloured pebbles and flowers are all perfect for the list, but be creative and add some more unusual items. Older kids may enjoy the extra competitive element of a time limit.

Treasure hunts

A treasure hunt would be a complete disappointment without an exciting treasure trove to uncover, so fill a small chest or box with foil-wrapped chocolate coins, marbles or other goodies that your kids love. Stow it out of sight, then put together a list of numbered clues that the kids have to solve and which will lead them to the treasure! Mark the numbers on tags, leaf-shaped bits of paper or rolled-up sheets of paper, and write the clues to the next number on the reverse. Hang clues from the lower branches of a tree, tuck them into gaps in the wall or hide them under pots. You can even have themed treasure hunts at special times of the year, such as an Easter egg hunt.

Plant bingo

This is a great way for your kids to learn about leaves. Put together a small grid on a sheet of paper and, in every square, draw the shape of a different leaf that can be found in your garden. Each leaf can be crossed out as it's found, and the first child to complete the grid is the winner.

garden games

While television, games systems and computers all have their place, encouraging children to play traditional games outdoors is good for their health and helps them to appreciate that the garden is not somewhere simply to grow plants, but somewhere they can have fun with their friends.

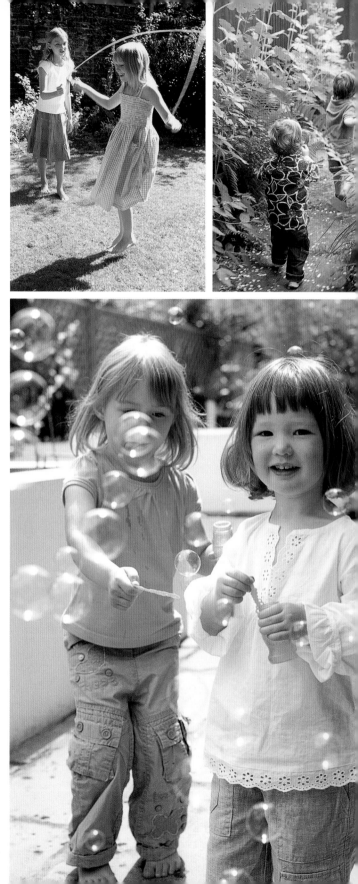

Fun and games

There are lots of games kids can play, whatever the size of garden. Even if you live in a flat or have a tiny outside space, there's no excuse – a public park is a perfect place for kids to burn off their energy.

Traditional games

Young children love to play scary games, such as 'What's the time, Mr Wolf?' Ask kids to draw straws or flip a coin to decide who will be Mr Wolf first. Mr Wolf stands at one end of the garden and turns his back on the rest of the group. Line the other children up at the opposite end of the garden. They shout, 'What's the time, Mr Wolf?'. The Wolf replies by saying 'One o'clock' or 'Nine o'clock', and so on, and the children take a step forward. When the Wolf says 'Dinner time', the kids run as the Wolf chases them. The child that is tagged then takes a turn at being the Wolf.

'Grandmother's Footsteps' is a variation on the 'Mr Wolf' theme. All the children try to creep up on Grandmother, who can turn round at any moment. When she does, the players must freeze. Anyone seen moving is sent back to the start line. The first child to reach Grandmother takes her place.

Letting off steam

Large gardens are perfect for ball games, races and chase games, such as tag, 'Stuck in the Mud' and 'Kick the Can', but smaller spaces also have plenty of potential for fun. Hopscotch doesn't take up much space, while skipping, French skipping or blowing big bubbles with soapy water can all be done in a garden the size of a postage stamp!

water play

There's no better way of cooling down on a long, hot summer's day than splashing about with water. There are lots of wet-play activies your kids can get stuck into, such as messing around with water pistols or racing boats in a paddling pool, but with a little bit of imagination you could invent some games of your own.

Car wash

On a sunny day, show the kids how to set up their very own back-garden car wash. Wheel out their bikes, tricycles or scooters from the garden shed, and line them up in a row. Now show your kids how to hose them down, using a bowl of soapy water and a scrubbing brush to remove any stubborn patches of dirt. If the children have plastic toys or a tea set, these can be swished around in a plastic bowl and left to dry out in the sun.

Water painting

Budding artists will enjoy getting stuck into water painting on a dry patio or path. It's easy, doesn't call for any special equipment and won't leave marks that are hard to clean off. All the kids need is a bowl of water and a paintbrush. Dip the brush into the water and encourage them to paint funny faces, strange creatures or pretty patterns. Alternatively, you could fill a used washing-up liquid bottle with water and your kids can squirt their name or a message onto the ground. If you have coloured chalks, let the kids get to work on their very own masterpieces, then have lots of fun washing them off later with a big bowl of soapy water.

Water tag

When friends come over, encourage the kids to let off steam by having a water fight or by playing water tag. All you need to do is soak a sponge in water and decide who's going to be 'it'. In turn, whoever they hit with the wet sponge becomes 'it'. So what are you waiting for? Grab them a towel, get their swimming costumes on and let the fun begin!

mini-beasts

If they carefully move stones, look under pieces of rotting wood or dig a shallow hole in the soil, children are likely to spot a mini-beast or two taking shelter or scavenging for food.

A backyard safari

Whether you live in the countryside or in the heart of the city, have rolling acres or a tiny plot, your garden will still be full of tiny creatures that can be tracked down by taking kids on a backyard safari.

Some of these creatures are instantly recognisable, such as slugs, snails, spiders, ladybirds, bees and butterflies. Others are less well known, but are becoming increasingly common, such as the metallic rosemary beetle, the crimson-coloured lily beetle or green shield bugs. This miniature insect kingdom is fascinating for children to explore, and if they look carefully they will find masses of different creatures in a matter of minutes.

Intrepid explorers

Although kids can head outdoors and start searching immediately, it's fun to put together an explorers' kit first.

It is easy to do and will help them remember everything they have seen. All they need is a cheap magnifying glass, a notebook and a pencil to record what they have seen. If they enjoy drawing, children could even try to sketch the mini-beasts they find. As their spotting skills develop, why not add a cheap digital camera to their kit? Kids will enjoy taking snaps of fast-moving or shy creatures, such as butterflies, which can later be downloaded onto a computer and then identified from the photo.

Identifying the beasts

There are many commonly found mini-beasts that are easy to identify, but children may discover a more unusual creature. A good book on garden wildlife, either borrowed from the library or bought from a shop, will help enormously when it comes to identifying the mini-beasts you've seen.

stockists and suppliers

CRAFT MATERIALS

B & Q
Visit www.diy.com for details of your nearest store.
Wide selection of terracotta plant pots and saucers, plus plants and seeds. Also masonry paint, ready-mixed tile grout and adhesive, plus gardening tools.

CALICO CRAFTS
www.calicocrafts.co.uk
Online crafts specialist with large stock of crafting materials.

CREATIONS ART AND CRAFTS MATERIALS
01326 555777
www.ecreations.co.uk
Online craft store with large stock of modelling clay, stencils, paints, brushes, glues and more.

EARLY LEARNING CENTRE
Call 0870 535 2352 or visit www.elc.co.uk for details of your nearest store.
Their craft section includes coloured paints, different-sized paintbrushes, felt-tip pens, plastic scissors, glue sticks, glitter pens and simple stencil designs in card and plastic. Also a selection of plastic first gardening tools that are good for younger children.

GREAT LITTLE TRADING CO.
Call 0870 850 6000 or visit www.gltc.co.uk for a catalogue.
Ready-mixed paint, art folders and 'paint-your-own' kits.

HOBBYCRAFT
Westway Cross Shopping Park
Greenford Road
London UB6 0UW
0800 027 2387
Visit www.hobbycraft.co.uk for details of your nearest store.
Chain of craft superstores carrying everything the young crafter needs: lollipop sticks, beads, bells, pompoms, balsa-wood packs, modelling clay, fabrics and felt.

HOMEBASE
Call 0845 077 8888 or visit www.homebase.co.uk for details of your nearest store.
Polished pebbles, masonry paint, ready-mixed tile grout and adhesive. Also a good selection of plain terracotta pots, bowls and saucers, which come in a range of sizes and are perfect for painting. Children's gardening tools are available seasonally, as well as a selection of colourful annuals and packet seeds.

HOMECRAFTS DIRECT
0116 269 7733
www.homecraftsdirect.co.uk
Established as a craft supplier for over 90 years, Homecrafts Direct claim to be the UK's largest arts-and-crafts suppliers. Log on to order hard-to-find items such as balsa wood and balsa cement, as well as craft staples such as crêpe paper, fabric paints, air-drying clay and instant papier-mâché mix.

LAKELAND LTD
Visit www.lakelandlimited.com to order a catalogue or for details of your nearest store.
Fantastic selection of crafting products available both in the mail-order catalogue and on the website, including a huge selection of decorative stamps and inks.

NORFOLK LAVENDER
0870 243 0147
www.norfolk-lavender.co.uk
Suppliers of bags of dried lavender, for making lavender bags, as well as cut stems of dried lavender, all available by mail order. Also a selection of lavender gifts and toiletries.

SELWYN-SMITH STUDIOS
148 High Street
Teddington
Middlesex TW11 8HZ
020 8973 0771
Paper, pens, pencils, paintbrushes and paint dishes.

URCHIN
Call 0870 112 6006 or visit www.urchin.co.uk to order a catalogue.
Bumper craft packs as well as craft kits that make great gifts.

WIMBLEDON SEWING & CRAFT SUPERSTORE
296–312 Balham High Road
London SW17 7AA
020 8767 0036
www.craftysewer.com
Everything from beads and sequins to blank cards, felt, pompoms, wool, buttons and pipe cleaners, lollipop sticks and craft sticks, and hessian fabric.

GARDENING TOOLS AND EQUIPMENT

BRIO
Visit www.brio.net for details of your nearest retailer.
Colourful, good-quality kids' garden tools that will last for years.

HABITAT
196–199 Tottenham Court Road, London W1T 7PJ
0844 499 1122
Call 870 411 5501 or visit www.habitat.net for details of your nearest store.
Cute kids' garden equipment.

HARROD HORTICULTURAL
www.harrodhorticultural.com
0845 402 5300
High-quality stainless-steel kids' tools that look just like the grown-up versions. Also Wellington boots, aprons and gloves.

IKEA
Visit www.ikea.com for a catalogue or for details of your nearest store.
Seasonal selection of gardening furniture, clay plant pots and other useful items.

JOHN LEWIS
Visit www.johnlewis.com for details of your nearest store.
A good seasonal selection of tools, watering cans and seeds for budding young gardeners.

JUST WILLIAMS
18 Half Moon Lane,
Herne Hill
London SE24 9HU
020 7733 9995
Traditional children's toyshop, with some child-size garden tools.

LETTERBOX
www.letterbox.co.uk
Plastic Peter Rabbit gardening tools
for younger children.

**NETHER WALLOP TRADING
COMPANY**
www.netherwalloptrading.com
Unusual and practical products for
the garden, such as a paper potter
tool to make pots from old
newspapers, jumbo oak plant
labels, a wildflower seed shaker and
biodegradable leaf sacks.

TIGER LILLY FLOWERS
020 8675 5454
www.tigerlillyflowers.co.uk
Florist selling fresh flowers,
bouquets, indoor and outdoor
plants, windchimes, and gifts, as
well as seasonal selection of ready-
made wreaths and Christmas trees.

WILKINSON SWORD
Call 01656 695595 or visit
www.wilkinsonswordgarden.com
for details of your nearest retailer.
Practical, durable kids' tools.

WOOLWORTHS
Visit www.woolworths.co.uk for
details of your nearest store.
Seasonal selection of gardening
items including children's tools,
Wellington boots, pots and seeds.

PLANTS

DELFLAND PLANTS
01354 740553
www.organicplants.co.uk
Vegetables, salads, herbs, fruit and
ornamentals, all of them organic.
Some fun varieties like chard 'Bright
Lights'.

GINKGO GARDEN CENTRE
Ravenscourt Park
London W6 0SL
020 8563 7112
www.ginkgogardens.co.uk
Plants, trees, shrubs, flowers, seeds
and more.

**HAMPSHIRE CARNIVOROUS
PLANTS**
023 8047 3314
www.hantsflytrap.com
Nursery specialising in carnivorous
plants, including a special
'Beginners' Collection'. Also suitable composts and other sundries.

**HOLLY GATE CACTUS
NURSERY**
Billingshurst Road
Ashington
West Sussex RH20 3BB
01903 892930
www.hollygatecactus.co.uk
Cacti and succulents.

HOMEBASE
Call 0845 077 8888 or visit
www.homebase.co.uk for your
nearest store.
DIY stores with a garden section
selling annuals and other plants.

J ARTHUR BOWERS
Visit www.william-sinclair.co.uk for
details of your nearest retailer.
Large selection of special and
general composts to suit different
plants and growing conditions. Also
plant foods, soil conditioners (such
as manure) and mulches.

JEKKA'S HERB FARM
Rose Cottage
Shellards Lane
Alveston
Bristol BS35 3SY
01454 418878
www.jekkasherbfarm.com
A specialist all-organic herb nursery.

KEN MUIR
0870 7479111
www.kenmuir.co.uk
Strawberries and many other soft
fruits, as well as fruit and nut trees.
Also a wide selection of minarettes
– tall, thin fruit trees that produce
fruit on small vertical branches
rather than growing horizontally.
Minarettes crop prolifically and can
be grown on balconies and patios.

MR FOTHERGILLS
01638 751161
www.mr-fothergills.co.uk
Huge selection of flower and
vegetable seeds.

NEAL'S NURSERY
0870 243 0147
www.capitalgardens.co.uk
Great selection of plants and seeds,
plus a variety of cute kid-sized
tools, gloves, rain capes, Wellington
boots, and garden baskets and
trugs in both traditional styles and
fun bright colours. Also stones,
pebbles and pots.

SUTTONS
0844 922 0606
www.suttons.co.uk
Flower and vegetable seeds, as
well as a special selection of child-
friendly seeds that will appeal to
kids and are easy to grow.

THOMPSON & MORGAN
01473 688821
www.thompson-morgan.com
Potato tubers and a large selection
of flower and vegetable seeds.

**WILDWOODS WATER
GARDENS**
Theobalds Park Road
Crews Hill
Enfield
Middlesex EN2 9BP
0208 366 0243
www.wildwoods.co.uk
Tufa rocks for the alpine garden
project.

**WYEVALE GARDEN
CENTRES**
Call 0800 413213 or visit
www.wyevale.co.uk for your nearest
garden centre.
Colourful annuals and other plants.

picture credits

2-3 Clothes from a selection at H&M (www.hm.com); trough from Ikea; plants from Ginkgo Garden Centre; wooden trowel from Neal's Nurseries; mini trug with tools from Habitat; plants from Woldens (www.betterplants.co.uk), Wyevale Garden Centres and Crews Hill Gardening Club (020 8367 9406); 4-5 hessian fabric for tote bag and plant labels from The Wimbledon Sewing & Craft Superstore; wooden trowel from Neal's Nurseries; 6-7 plant pots from Homebase; mini trug with tools from Habitat; annual plants from Homebase; 8-9 mini trug with tools from Habitat; 10-11 pots from Homebase; compost pots from Neal's Nurseries; clothes from H&M (www.hm.com); 12-13 rakes, gloves, spade and dibber from Neal's Nurseries; mini trug with tools from Habitat; wellies from a selection at Sainsburys and Woolworths; 14-15 rake and spade from Neal's Nurseries; 16-17 spade and trowel from Neal's Nurseries; watering can from John Lewis; 18-19 glass jars from a selection at Muji (www.muji.co.uk); clothes from H&M (www.hm.com); seeds and tray courtesy of Martyn Cox; 20-21 terracotta pots from Homebase; paper potter tool from Nether Wallop Trading Company; paper for pots from Cowling & Wilcox (www.cowlingandwilcox.com); 22-23 terracotta pots from Homebase; plastic scissors from Early Learning Centre; 24-25 wooden dowelling for scarecrow from B&Q; 26-27 watering can from John Lewis; star patterned beaker from Cath Kidston (www.cathkidston.co.uk); wood plant labels from The Wimbledon Sewing and Craft Superstore; 28-29 paper potter tool from Nether Wallop Trading Company; 30-31 window box and herbs from B&Q; 32-33 plastic scissors from Early Learning Centre; cellophane bag from Lakeland Ltd; gingham ribbon from The Wimbledon Sewing & Craft Superstore; 34-35 glass pots from IKEA; egg cups from John Lewis; large lollipop sticks from The Wimbledon Sewing & Craft Superstore;

36-37 metal dustbin from IKEA; compost from J Arthur Bowers; potatoes from Thompson & Morgan; 38-39 woven hanging basket, plants and herbs from a selection at Wyevale Garden Centres, Homebase and B&Q; compost by J Arthur Bowers; watering can from John Lewis; 40-41 strawberry planter from Homebase; strawberry plants from B&Q; watering can from John Lewis; clothes from H&M (www.hm.com); 42-43 star-patterned plastic beakers from Cath Kidston (www.cathkidston.co.uk); plants from Crews Hill Gardening Club (020 8367 9406); 44-45 cupcakes from Waitrose (www.waitrose.com); 46-47 terracotta bowl from Homebase; glass pots from IKEA; paintbrushes from The Wimbledon Sewing & Craft Superstore; compost from Homebase; 48-49 cacti from Neal's Nurseries; plastic animals and figures from Toys R Us (www.toysrus.com); bowl and white gravel both from Homebase; 50-51 alpine plants from Browns Garden Centre (www.brownsgardencentre.co.uk); compost from Homebase; wooden cows from Just Williams; watering can from John Lewis; 52-53 terracotta pots from Homebase; grit from Wyevale Garden Centres; compost from Homebase; sempervivums from Crews Hill Gardening Club (020 8367 9406); 54-55 animals from Toys R Us (www.toysrus.co.uk); charcoal from Enfield Bird Centre; plants from Homebase/Wyevale Garden Centres; clay pellets from Homebase; compost from J Arthur Bowers; 56-57 bamboo canes from B&Q; rake from Neal's Nurseries; 58-59 watering can from John Lewis; bamboo canes from B&Q; 60-61 pot from Homebase; plants from Browns Garden Company (www.brownsgardencentre.co.uk), Wyevale and Crews Hill Gardening Club (020 8367 9406); compost from Thompsons of Crews Hill (www.thompsonsofcrewshill.com); 62-63 felt, pipecleaners and miniature pompoms from The Wimbledon Sewing & Craft Superstore; 64-65 terracotta

pots and gerbera plants from Homebase; clothes from H&M (www.hm.com); 66-67 birdbox from Neal's Nurseries; lollipop sticks from Hobbycraft; 68-70 lollipop sticks from Hobbycraft; large lollipop sticks from The Wimbledon Sewing & Craft Superstore; 70-71 felt, miniature pompoms and pipecleaners from The Wimbledon Sewing & Craft Superstore; 72-73 flower press from Lakeland Ltd; plants from Ginkgo Garden Centre; basket from Neal's Nurseries; 74-75 terracotta saucer, pebbles and waterproof adhesive and grout from Homebase; 76-77 raffia from Hobbycraft; 78-79 felt and pipecleaners from The Wimbledon Sewing & Craft Superstore; 80-81 hessian, fusible interlining and embroidery cottons all from The Wimbledon Sewing & Craft Superstore; 82-83 as above; wood plant labels from The Wimbledon Sewing & Craft Superstore; trowel from Neal's Nurseries; 84-85 loose lavender from The Norfolk Lavender Company; fabrics from a selection at Cath Kidston (www.cathkidston.co.uk); embroidery threads from The Wimbledon Sewing & Craft Superstore; clothes by H&M (www.hm.com); 86-87 bias binding and calico fabric for apron from The Wimbledon Sewing & Craft Superstore; fabric paint from The Stencil Library; watering can from John Lewis; basket from Neal's Nurseries; plants from Ginkgo Garden Centre; 88-89 glass jars from IKEA; beads from The Wimbledon Sewing & Craft Superstore; windchime (used for pieces) from Tiger Lilly Flowers; 90-91 as above; 92-93 envelopes from a selection at Rymans; raffia from Hobbycraft; 94-95 brown paper from IKEA; raffia from Hobbycraft; card tags from Rymans; clothes from H&M (www.hm.com); 96-97 string from Homebase; birdseed from Neal's Nurseries; 98-99 wire from The Wimbledon Sewing & Craft Superstore; raffia from Hobbycraft; 100-101 colander from IKEA; clothes from H&M (www.hm.com); 102-103 clothes from

H&M (www.hm.com); pumpkin from Kennards Good Foods (57 Lamb's Conduit Street, London WC1N 3NB, 020 7404 4030); 104-105 wooden dowelling for scarecrow frame from B&Q; hessian from The Wimbledon Sewing & Craft Superstore; 106-107 as above; 108-109 twig wreath from a selection at Tiger Lilly Flowers; gingham ribbon from The Wimbledon Sewing & Craft Superstore; 110-111 twig wreath from a selection at Tiger Lilly Flowers; gold and silver paint from The Wimbledon Sewing & Craft Superstore; gold ribbon from Hobbycraft; 112-113 silver paint from The Wimbledon Sewing & Craft Superstore; 114-115 Wellington boots from a selection at Sainsburys (www.sainsburys.co.uk) and Woolworths; 116-117 chocolate coins from Selfridges (www.selfridges.com); 118-119 bubble mixture from Tesco (www.tesco.com); 120-121 watering can from John Lewis.

index

acknowledgments

Thank you to Polly Wreford for her beautiful photography and attention to detail. Thanks also to Iona Hoyle and Annabel Morgan for their help with all stages of the book – design, layout and words.

Thank you to all the fantastic children who modelled for the book – for their patience during photography, and their enthusiasm for the projects they worked on.

Thanks also to the Norfolk Lavender Company for supplying the lavender, and to J. Arthur Bowers for supplying the composts used in the projects.

Catherine Woram

Thank you Alis, Louis and Lily.

Martyn Cox

Ryland Peters & Small would like to thank all the children who modelled in this book: Ahana; Bella; Carmel; Charlotte; Ella; Ella; Ivo and Honor; Georgia; Giorgia; Harry and India; Grace; Gregory; Harriet; Havana and Hassia; Isaac; James and Ben; James; Jessica and Anna; Jordan; Joseph; Kaan; Katie; Kinquaid; Lily; Louis; Miles and Caspar; Millie and Arthur; Sam and Roddy; Saskia and Mia; Sebastian and Oliver; and Tahiti.

Many thanks also to those who kindly allowed us to photograph in their gardens, especially Victoria Hutton and Patricia Woram.